The
Condo
Book

How to Avoid Getting Burned When Buying and Living in a Home within a Community Association

DAVID T. SCHWINDT, CPA, RS, PRA
Schwindt & Co.
Certified Public Accountants and Consultants

BEYOND WORDS
Hillsboro, Oregon

BEYOND WORDS
20827 N.W. Cornell Road, Suite 500
Hillsboro, Oregon 97124-9808
503-531-8700 / 503-531-8773 fax
www.beyondword.com

First Beyond Words trade paperback edition March 2016

Beyond Words Publishing is an imprint of Simon & Schuster, Inc., and the Beyond Words logo is a registered trademark of Beyond Words Publishing, Inc.

For more information about special discounts for bulk purchases, please contact Beyond Words Special Sales at 503-531-8700 or specialsales@beyondwords.com.

Manufactured in the United States of America

10 9 8 7 6 5 4 3 2 1

Library of Congress Control Number: 2016933918

ISBN 978-1-58270-582-8

ISBN 978-1-58270-583-5 (ebook)

The corporate mission of Beyond Words Publishing, Inc.: *Inspire to Integrity*

This book is dedicated to my children, Sarah and Stephen, who are a constant inspiration to me, as well as to the outstanding team of professionals at Schwindt & Co. and our HOA clients who have given us an abundance of good feedback over the years.

Contents

Contents

Preface

E arly in my accounting career, I was introduced to condominium and homeowners associations through an affiliation with an office-sharing CPA who needed help auditing an association. This was in 1984. As I learned more about associations and this industry, I became intrigued with the nuances not only with accounting, budgeting, and tax issues but also with governance and ongoing maintenance of association properties. This was the start of a life-long learning process that began with the formation of Schwindt & Co. in 1989, a full-service CPA firm located in Portland, Oregon, specializing in providing accounting and tax services and reserve studies and consulting with over five hundred condominium and homeowners associations in the Pacific Northwest. Our firm of over fifteen professionals acts as a resource in many areas of accounting, governance, budgeting, and tax consulting.

Over thirty years of experience have been brought to bear in creating this book—that experience includes specialized training in the fields of accounting, auditing, taxation, and reserve-study preparation. There are many publications devoted to certain aspects of condominium and homeowners associations. This book integrates numerous concepts and acts as a resource for buyers, sellers, board members, community industry professionals, and members of associations alike.

Inadequate training and dissemination of information and best practices are the limiting factors in most associations, preventing them from operating as vibrant, successful organizations. It is my hope that this book may help foster understanding and harmony within associations and provide a blueprint for successful associations.

Introduction

I like surprises.

A gift from a loved one, one's son or daughter accomplishing something special, a visit from an old friend. These are nice surprises.

I like condominiums.

Condominiums are relatively inexpensive, require very little property maintenance by the individual unit owners, and often have other amenities such as clubhouses, swimming pools, and tennis courts.

What I don't like are condominium surprises.

Condominium surprises generally mean drama, that I need to write a check I'd really rather not write, or that I have to live with something that may adversely affect my quality of life.

This book helps to avoid financial and other surprises when buying a condominium or a single-family home within an association. *The Condo Book* is also a resource to help understand best practices within the community and provide ways to foster community in order to enhance the living experience of all members.

In this book, I explore:

- Ways to avoid making a costly mistake when buying a condominium or single-family home within an association
- Discussion of the similarities and differences among condominiums, single-family home associations, cooperatives, timeshares, manufactured home parks, and intentional (cohousing) communities
- Tips on implementing best practices within an association
- Tips on how to create community within an association to foster a better lifestyle for all members
- Suggestions for further reading in each subject area

Home ownership within an association has skyrocketed in the last twenty years. Even though the housing market in some areas of the country is still struggling to work its way out of the recession, the shortage of properties has buyers scrambling to find suitable housing. Soon builders will begin building new condominiums again.

This book speaks primarily to condominium associations.* I believe condominiums are a wonderful way to maximize your housing dollars and, under the right circumstances, can provide both a great lifestyle and a wise investment. However, the days of banking on rising condominium prices and ensuring that anyone buying a condominium will see a good rate of return on an investment are over—at least in the foreseeable future. This is not meant to be discouraging or depressing, merely realistic. Today's buyer needs to be more sophisticated than ever to avoid costly mistakes in buying a condominium. It is the goal of this book to help you become the most savvy, sophisticated buyer you can be in today's buyers' climate.

As is detailed in the pages to come, many condominium associations are in dire financial straits brought on by underfunded reserves; improperly maintained common property such as roofs, siding, and windows; and general mismanagement. With the real-estate meltdown in 2007, many homeowners ran into financial difficulty and were not able to pay monthly condominium assessments. This has led to cash flow shortages for many associations. To continue operating, associations in many instances reduced the required contributions to reserves and did not pay for ongoing maintenance procedures on common area properties. The challenge for buyers of

---

*Please note that many associations consist of single-family homes with amenities such as clubhouses, swimming pools, and tennis courts. Also, legal entities discussed later in this book, such as cooperatives and timeshares, share many characteristics with condominiums. The issues for single-family home associations, timeshares, and cooperatives are often the same as those for condominiums in that the associations are generally charged with repairing, replacing, and maintaining common area property (clubhouses, swimming pools, etc.) and, therefore, many of the same pitfalls exist.

Introduction

condominiums today is that the warning signs of financial problems are not always readily apparent—the worst-case scenario is that a new buyer finds out a year or two after purchase that a *special assessment* (see chapter 2 for more on special assessments) is needed to satisfy the financial needs of the association.

Many associations put off addressing these financial needs until it is too late, and whoever owns a home at the time of crisis has to pay in order to correct years of financial mismanagement. In many cases, associations play a costly game of financial musical chairs. What does this mean for you? Depending on when you buy your condominium, you could be doing so right after a series of costly projects requiring a special assessment. At this point, you have dodged a major financial bullet. However, if the culture of the association is not to fund reserves (discussed in chapter 16), the next time there is a major project and you still own the condominium, you will be required to pay for that special assessment.

This book will help you discern the financial health of each association and other common pitfalls to avoid in buying a condominium, enabling you to head off these sorts of problems before they become your problems to solve. The goal of this book is not to turn you into an expert in all areas of condominium ownership and management. I have been working in the condominium industry for over thirty years, and I am constantly learning new concepts. Think of this book as a primer that gives you the basics of homeowners and condominium association concepts, complete with overviews on key subjects of ownership, maintenance, and community building; end-of-chapter takeaways, best practices, tips, and further reading; and robust appendices to further support the often complex topics covered.

My goal is to help prevent you from entering what some like to call "condo hell" and to provide tips to improve the overall quality of life within your association when you do decide to buy. So, when do you know you are in condo hell?

- You are hit with a $3,000 special assessment six months after purchase.
- Your condominium fees double within one year.
- Your unit starts leaking, and the association discovers construction defects.
- You are caught in the middle of a power struggle between your neighbors and the board of directors of the association, which leads to a lawsuit and a special assessment to pay for legal fees.
- You have been told new rules now prohibit your thirty-pound dog on the property.
- Your neighbors are not paying their dues, so your dues are going up.
- You discover you cannot rent your unit because rules permit only a certain percentage of rentals.
- You try to sell your unit, but your buyer cannot qualify for an FHA (Federal Housing Administration) loan because your association has not qualified for FHA certification.
- You learn the association treasurer has embezzled funds and, as a result, your dues dramatically increase.
- Your neighbors harass you, and your association does nothing.
- The building and grounds look terrible six months after purchase, and the board says there is no money to properly maintain the property.

This list could go on, but I have a feeling you get the general idea.

Is there a "condo heaven"? I work with many harmonious associations that are well managed and have adequate reserves to pay for all future repairs and maintenance with little likelihood of major increases in assessments or the possibility of a special assessment. I salute those associations that adhere to best practices and strive to create harmonious and financially responsible communities.

It is my hope that this book helps you find one of these wonderful communities to call your home.

1

What Am I Really Buying?

When purchasing a condominium, you are obviously buying the interior space of your condominium (except in the case of a cooperative, which will be discussed in chapter 23). You are also buying a pro rata* share of the common property, including the roof, siding, decks, asphalt, swimming pools, and clubhouse.

The members within the condominium association own this common area property. The association has the responsibility of maintaining, repairing, and replacing this property and is also responsible for governing the activities of the association, which includes enforcing the provisions of the governing document and rules and regulations established by the association. As the buyer, you are also assuming the financial responsibility as a member of the association. The ongoing costs of managing may include insurance, landscaping,

---

* *Pro rata* is defined as an individual member's share of the total amount of expenditures for operating the association and savings for necessary future repairs and maintenance. This pro rata share is generally defined by the governing documents and could be an equal amount shared by all members based on square footage of the units or a combination.

management fees, utilities, et cetera. If this sounds a lot like a partnership with the other members, it is—at least in practical terms.

Let me be clear: you are not only buying your unit, you are also buying into a quasi-general partnership with people you do not know. How does that sound? A little scary? You're not alone if you think so. Added to that, you are also likely turning over all the decisions of operating the organization to a board of directors—also people you may not know and who may or may not be qualified. Also, the board members sometimes have agendas to further their positions of authority on the board. These could range from keeping dues artificially low to controlling architectural review procedures.

Suppose I came to you and asked you to buy into an organization that obligated you to pay any deficiency that organization currently has or may have in the future. What would you need to know before making a decision? Would you blindly buy into the organization hoping that nothing bad will happen, or would you feel obliged to perform due diligence before signing your name on the line? I hope you would choose the latter.

When purchasing a condominium, you employ realtors, appraisers, lenders, and home inspectors and may obtain warranties from the seller. While professionals have their place in the process of buying, the experts noted may not have the skillsets to provide you with all the information you need to determine the overall financial health of the association or the state of the politics within the association, nor would they likely want the liability of attempting to do so.

What's a buyer to do? You could hire attorneys, association community managers, or certified public accountants (CPAs) to analyze the association. However, after spending hundreds or even thousands of dollars on consultants, you may decide not purchase the condominium.

Before you hire anyone, you need to know the right questions to ask. Throughout this book, I discuss the type of information you need to collect, and I help you focus your questions. Then, should you hire an attorney, CPA, or other expert, you will be focused and efficient, helping you get more satisfactory answers and avoiding unnecessary costs.

I've also found that numerous articles written on how to successfully buy a condominium do not provide adequate information, giving buyers a false sense of security. As an example, many lending agencies require associations to contribute a minimum of 10 percent of the total assessments to replacement reserves, a savings account that funds future repairs and maintenance, such as replacing roofs.* This level of contribution is usually too low to adequately fund reserves (this subject is more fully explained in chapter 16).

When buying a condominium, buyers normally compare several properties that are relatively close in price. Too often and with no other information, buyers naively look to the level of association fees and assume the lowest fee is the best. The problem is that buyers may not have sufficient information to interpret what the fees actually represent.

The key to making an informed decision about buying a condominium or single-family home within an association is dependent on having the right information, knowing how to analyze that information, and knowing the right questions to ask the appropriate person. Without this information and process, a buyer is

---

*This requirement may not take into consideration whether the association has been contributing an adequate amount throughout the years. What if the association just started contributing 10 percent, which may be inadequate to begin with? The association could be dramatically under-reserved, which means when it is time to pay for a major repair, such as a new roof, there may not be enough money in the reserve fund. Generally, this means that the association will be forced to special-assess the members. Depending on where you are on this timeline, you could be faced with a special assessment shortly after purchasing a condominium. Most purchasers maximize an investment by putting as much as they can toward a down payment and then spend their remaining funds furnishing the condominium. If you are special-assessed when you cannot afford to pay the assessment, the association will charge late fees for not paying, thus compounding the problem.

making a decision with inadequate facts and could make a poor decision—especially when comparing multiple properties. This book is designed to give you tools for acquiring the right information, with tips on how to analyze this information in order to make an informed decision.

Chapter Takeaways

- When buying a condominium, remember that you are buying not only your unit but also a pro rata share of the building and amenities.
- You and your neighbors are responsible for the financial and maintenance needs of the association for as long as you own your unit.
- Management responsibilities resides with the board of directors, which may or may not be doing an effective job. Keep in mind that the board consists of people from all walks of life who purchased a property within an association and, thus, found themselves with the responsibilities of managing an entity that is, in essence, a small business. New board members may not undergo a training process to qualify them to make sound decisions on behalf of the members, and prospective or existing members should take care to effectively analyze the operations of the association to ensure that there are no surprises.
- The usual experts in a purchase—realtors, appraisers, lenders, and home inspectors—may not have the expertise to tell you if the association is properly managed and financially sound. Although these experts provide a valuable service in their respective areas of expertise, they often lack the specific knowledge to adequately analyze the operations of the association to assist you in determining if you are making a good decision.

Again, the key to making the best decision when buying a condominium or single-family home within an association rests with having the right information and knowing how to interpret and analyze this information.

- Looking at the level of fees of two similar condominiums gives you no information as to which one, if either, is collecting the proper amount of assessments and is financially sound. It is tempting to use the monthly condominium fees as a basis for making a decision. These monthly fees are used in determining eligibility of qualifying for a mortgage and can affect personal monthly cash flow. The saying *penny wise and pound foolish* comes to mind in situations like these. A buyer may believe he or she is saving money when purchasing a home with a low monthly association assessment. However, if the association is in financial trouble because it is not charging enough to its members on a monthly basis, sooner or later the association will need to assess the members enough to pay for needed operations or repairs and replacements. This could come in the form of a major increase in monthly assessments or in the form of a monthly or one-time special assessment.

Tips—Best Practices

Knowledgeable members of associations can greatly contribute to the success of the association. When buying a unit, enlisting the help of qualified professionals will assist you in sorting through the financial structure and practices of the association. You can then move forward knowing that the community is on a sound financial basis or aware of what issues you may be facing in the future, allowing you to adjust your offer or withdraw in a timely manner.

Tips—Creating Community

Sharing your knowledge of an association's best practices with other members can help create a more harmonious community.

Further Reading

To get started, I recommend reading various Community Associations Institute publications. These can be viewed and ordered at CAIonline.org under the "Information & Tools" section.

2

Terms Used in This Book

These terms will aid in analyzing documents and the affairs of your association. This list is not all-inclusive, but it will give you a basis for understanding the concepts in later chapters. Feel free to refer back to this chapter whenever necessary as you read on.

- **Accrual basis:** this is a method of accounting that recognizes receivables and payables as well as prepaid expenses, which allows the matching of expenses to appropriate periods. This method is approved by generally accepted accounting principles and represents the highest level of presenting the financial position of the association as of a specific date and the results of operations (income and expenses) for a specific time period.

- **Architectural control provisions:** these are rules detailed in the governing documents or rules adopted by the board of directors concerning how your unit or home can look, including paint colors. For example, there may be a rule prohibiting hardwood floors due to sound transmission to the unit below. Single-family home associations may have rules prohibiting painting residences other than earth-tone colors. Unless the governing documents permit, the board of directors may adopt rules that you do not agree with and you may not have power to change.

- **Architectural review committee:** known by many names, including art jury, design review committee, and environmental control committee, this committee is the one committee that is almost always set out in the CC&Rs (Covenants, Conditions, and Restrictions) or the bylaws. Its purpose is to ensure compliance with aesthetic standards established by the association. In a condominium, it is primarily focused on alterations and improvements that impact the common areas, window treatments visible from the outside, and balconies and patios.

- **Articles of incorporation:** this is a legal filing that limits the members of the association to a proportional share of obligations. Absent this status, each member may be liable for a judgment against the association in its entirety. Most states require that corporations renew their status annually; if they do not, the status may be suspended.

- **Association culture:** a culture of undocumented policies and procedures developed over time that the association members support could include best practices or practices that are detrimental to the members and prospective buyers (e.g., not funding reserves).

- **Audited, reviewed, and compiled financial statements:** financial statements prepared by an independent CPA in accordance with generally accepted accounting principles are differentiated by the level of assurance given by the CPA with concern to the accuracy of the information.

- **Bad debts:** when members do not pay their dues, this creates account-entitled bad debts. This shortfall in cash should be taken into account when budgeting and forces those members who do pay their assessments to pay more to make up for those not paying. When some members do not pay their dues, the other members who are paying on time are forced to make up the difference and pay a higher level of assessments.

- **Balance sheet:** this is a statement that lists assets and liabilities of the association as well as the fund's balance (the difference between assets and liabilities).

- **Board meeting:** the bylaws discuss when board meetings are to be held. Most associations hold monthly board meetings to discuss association business and pass resolutions on matters before the board. Most state statutes require associations to give advance notice to members regarding association meetings.

- **Board of directors:** members are elected by the membership to serve in a fiduciary capacity to manage the affairs of the association. Powers, responsibilities, terms of office, and other duties are outlined in the bylaws.

- **Bylaws:** this document spells out how the association is governed, how budgets are prepared, duties of the board of directors, and more. All bylaws are written differently.

- **Cash basis:** this is a method of accounting that recognizes transactions when cash is received and checks are issued. This method does not recognize receivables (amounts owed to the association), payables (amounts owed by the association to vendors), or prepaid expenses. This method is not considered to be an approved method by generally accepted accounting principles because the omission of receivables and payables may materially distort the financial position of the association.

- **CC&Rs** (Covenants, Conditions, and Restrictions): these are also referred to as governing documents. This is a broad description of association documents that normally include the declaration and bylaws. All documents are written uniquely to that association; just because you have read the declaration and bylaws of one condominium doesn't mean it applies to another condominium.

- **Committee meeting:** meetings held by various committees include finance, architectural review, and social. Minutes of these meetings are generally available to members.
- **Common-area components:** these are components the association is responsible for replacing, maintaining, and repairing and typically include but are not limited to the roof, siding, windows, doors, clubhouse, swimming pool, and asphalt. The declaration usually describes these components.
- **Complete building envelope inspection:** an inspection performed by a qualified engineering or architectural firm takes into consideration design, materials, and workmanship of the common area components and may include intrusive openings around windows and decks. The purpose of a complete building envelope inspection is to give the association information on the present condition of common area components. This may lead to issues relating to construction defects.
- **Condominium association:** this is a legal entity created by the developer, governed by state statutes and the CC&Rs, and incorporated in the state of residence. The association may include condominium units, townhouse units, and commercial units.
- **Condominium conversions:** conversions are often apartments subsequently converted to condominiums. These projects have special issues depending on the extent of refurbishment performed by the developer during the conversion process.
- **Construction defects:** defects of common area property as a result of substandard design, materials, or workmanship may cause water intrusion, dry rot, and other issues that may result in costly repairs.
- **Cooperative:** this is a form of ownership very common in large metro areas. The co-op owns the building and all of the units.

Members buy a pro rata interest in the property. Qualifying to become a member of a co-op can be demanding because the co-op board has the right to refuse a sale based on subjective criteria.

- **Declarant:** this is the legal name given to the developer. When reading documents, be aware that the declarant has special rights and responsibilities. Declarants are involved with new condominiums and condominium conversions.

- **Declaration:** this is a document that, among other things, spells out who owns the property and to what proportion the owner-ship of this property resides with each owner. All declarations are written differently, so keep in mind that just because you have read the declaration of one condominium doesn't mean what you've read applies to another condominium.

- **Due diligence:** this is the work purchasers should accomplish when analyzing the association. This process will not be complete until all available information is received to make an informed decision. It is likely that not all requested information will be received. In this case, the decision will involve the consideration of missing information.

- **Executive session board meeting:** this is a closed session with only board members present. It is convened during a regular board meeting to discuss certain employment issues, contracts with vendors, or existing, pending, or threatened litigation. The discussion in executive session is confidential. However, when the board reconvenes after an executive session, there is usually a decision resulting from the closed-door discussion. The presence of executive sessions may mean the association is involved in an issue that is out of the ordinary and perhaps of concern.

- **Faction group:** this is a group of members who oppose the current board of directors and wish to assert their agenda on the association. This type of group can cause discord in the association and may lead to lawsuits between the faction group and the association. You should not assume that the faction group is wrong or that the board is wrong in the disputed matter. It may be that both are right, and it is a matter of philosophy. In any case, if emotions are running strong, it may result in drama and attorney fees. Faction groups can highlight areas of association management that need attention. If a board pays attention to the issues raised by faction groups and takes steps toward addressing these issues, this can result in a positive outcome for the association.

- **Fee simple/leasehold ownership:** most ownership of condominiums, townhomes, and single-family homes are "fee simple," which means the owners or members either have a pro rata interest in the land or an outright ownership. Many condominiums in Hawaii are sold with a leasehold interest in the land—this means that the owner, via a pro rata interest in the land, does not own the land. Rather, the owner is leasing the land until a predetermined date.

- **Homeowners association:** this is the same as a condominium association except the association includes free-standing single-family residences with common property such as a clubhouse, roads, tennis courts, et cetera. Townhouse-style units could be classified as a homeowners association as opposed to a condominium association. Single-family homeowners associations are responsible for the grounds; individual owners are responsible for the exterior of their residences.

- **In-house financial statements:** financial statements prepared by a bookkeeper, the treasurer of the association, or the management company include a balance sheet, a statement of revenue and expenses, and a variance report.

- **Lawsuit:** this is a legal action instigated by the board representing the association, or outside parties or owners instituting action against the association.

- **Letter to those charged with governance (management letter):** this is a letter written to the board of directors by the certified public accountant recommending changes to the policies, procedures, and internal controls.
- **Limited common area components:** this is same as common area components except access is restricted to specific parties. An example is a deck that is maintained by the association, but access is only available to the condominium owner. The repair and maintenance of these components may be the responsibility of the association or the member.
- **Maintenance plan:** this plan specifies certain procedures to protect and extend the useful lives of common area components. Typical procedures include keeping the roof free of debris and moss, cleaning out the gutters, caulking around doors and windows, and regularly inspecting on the property to determine if any components need attention.
- **Minutes:** this is a written record of business transacted at a board meeting. Some minutes are voluminous but detailed minutes may give you valuable information.
- **Operating budget:** this budget is prepared by either the property manager or the board and approved according to the governing documents. Generally it includes expenses that occur monthly or yearly, such as insurance, landscaping, utilities, and management fees.
- **Professionally managed:** an associations that hires a professional association manager to manage the affairs of the association is professionally managed. This may include accounting and management.
- **Punch list:** this list is given to the developer by a purchaser of a condominium to fix certain construction issues on the inside of a unit. This may include squeaky floors and cosmetic issues. These costs are usually not the responsibility of the association.

- **Reserve study/replacement reserve budget:** a cash flow budget includes all expenditures relating to replacement, repair, and maintenance of common area components that generally occur from two to thirty years in the future. Replacement items include but are not limited to roof, siding and windows, painting, and asphalt seal coating.
- **Rules and regulations:** these are rules that are not included in state statutes, declarations, or bylaws. These are not always codified and distributed to members. They carry fines if not obeyed. An example is "no dogs in excess of twenty-five pounds are allowed."
- **Self-managed:** some associations elect to perform all association functions themselves in lieu of hiring an association management company. This includes hiring on-site management and accounting personnel.
- **Special assessment:** an assessment over and above regular monthly assessments normally involves a financial surprise when the association discovers there are not sufficient funds to pay for needed expenses, repairs, or litigation.
- **State statutes:** statutory laws govern associations. Most states separate these laws between condominiums and single-family home associations since the attributes of each can be different. Depending on the type of unit you are considering buying, care should be taken to address the correct statutes.
- **Statement of revenue and expenses:** this statement lists revenue and expenses for a given time period.
- **Timeshare:** this form of ownership involves owning or having a beneficial right to use a condominium on a specified week(s) during a year. Such a right may include the opportunity to trade a specified week for a different week in the same complex or for a complex in a different part of the world.

- **Turnover:** this event transfers the control of the association from the declarant to a board of directors elected by the membership. This happens in accordance with the governing documents after 75 percent of the units are sold.
- **Variance report:** this statement lists the statement of revenue and expenses for a specific time period compared to the approved budget. The variance is the difference between the budget and the actual income or expense for each budget line item. This statement can be a valuable tool to ascertain if the association is collecting and spending money in accordance with the annual budget approved by the board of directors.

3

Buying a Condominium: Dispelling Myths

There is a great deal of misinformation used by purchasers as a basis for not performing proper due diligence when buying a condominium. These beliefs stem from the fact that many professionals are involved in the purchase and closing of properties. They also include the assumption that a layperson will know if there are issues involving the purchase. The following are typical myths prospective buyers and owners should watch out for.

Myth #1: My realtor will let me know if the association is in trouble.

Realtors perform a wonderful service for their clients. They help locate properties; perform a comparable sales analysis to determine if the listing price is reasonable; help negotiate the purchase; help facilitate the inspection; and assist with providing information to the buyer. Realtors may know a lot about the neighborhoods, schools, and other criteria important to the purchaser. However, they are not generally experts when it comes to analyzing the physical and financial status of the association.

Realtors often will not know what information is needed to make an informed decision about buying into an association. How to obtain documents such as reserve studies, financial statements, minutes of the board of directors meetings, and CC&Rs may not be in the realtor's repertoire. Think of your realtor as a trusted professional on whom you can rely to obtain some information for your analysis. When selecting a realtor, you should make sure he or she understands the issues covered in this book.

Bottom line: *Realtors can help you analyze the association, but do not depend on the realtor to determine if you are buying into an association in trouble.*

Myth #2: I am having my condo inspected by a certified home inspector. If anything is wrong with my unit or the common area property, the inspector will let me know.

Property inspectors perform a valuable service. They can alert you of potential issues with the interior of your unit and issues relating to the exterior of your building. Keep in mind that the inspection report ranges between $250 and $450, and the liability of the inspector is almost always limited to the fee. For an inspector, the main objective is to evaluate the condominium unit or single-family home, not the common area property, which includes *all* of the buildings, grounds, clubhouse, and amenities.

Bottom line: *Do not depend on the home inspector to alert you to issues relating to all common area property. That person's main concern is the condition of your unit.*

As detailed in chapter 17, it may be possible to employ the home inspector you hire to inspect your unit to also walk the common area of the association and give you an idea if he or she thinks the association is properly maintaining the property. Please keep in mind that this may be for an extra charge and do not expect a report since this is out of the scope of the inspection of the unit or single-family home.

Myth #3: The condominium appraised for more than I am paying, so I am good to go.

Appraisals are based on comparable sales to like property. They rarely take into consideration the financial health of the association. It is possible to have two condominium associations identical in size, location, amenities, and age, yet one association could be in sound financial health and the other on the brink of financial ruin.

The appraisal would most likely show that both condominiums are of comparable value, because most valuations are based on a comparable sales price per square foot of similar properties. At that moment, the appraisal may be correct. But as soon as the special assessment is in effect or dues increase dramatically, sales prices will drop for the troubled association. Which condominium would you want to buy?

Bottom line: *Do not depend on the appraisal to give you information on the financial health of the association.* There are many other ways to determine the financial health of the association that can be found throughout this book. The point here is to place credence on the right information.

Myth #4: I have asked the seller to disclose any issues with the condo, including if that person is aware of a pending special assessment or other important issues to be considered, so if there were an issue, I would know.

Sellers are obligated to disclose knowledge of special assessments or financial matters that may be detrimental to purchasers. However, most sellers are not paying attention to the ongoing management of the association. Thus, they would not be aware of impending special assessments, lawsuits, construction defects, and other matters that may be important in making a decision to buy. Even if the seller is on the board of directors, the board may not be using best practices to understand potential issues. Do not place all of your faith in seller representations.

Bottom line: *Do not depend on the seller to disclose financial issues relating to the association. Even though you may not be able to depend on seller disclosures, there are other ways to uncover hidden issues as discussed throughout the book. Many sellers are not paying attention to the affairs of the association and may not be a good resource for information.*

Myth #5: I have viewed the property, and the buildings look like they are in great condition, so I should not have any problems.

Engineers and architects like to show before and after pictures of a condominium building that looks beautiful in the first picture. The second picture shows the same building with the siding torn off and the building covered in dry rot. Even experts sometimes have difficulty determining if a building is in good shape in terms of design, materials, and workmanship. Unless the building has undergone a *complete building envelope inspection* (see chapter 2), it is often difficult to know if you are buying a ticking time bomb leading to a construction defect event and a special assessment.

Bottom line: *Do not depend on your impression of how the buildings and grounds look. Perform due diligence and investigate past the "face" of the property. See the definition of* due diligence *in chapter 2.*

Myth #6: The condo fees are lower than most associations', so the board must be doing a better job of managing the association, and it's better for me financially.

Associations that keep assessments artificially low may be foregoing ongoing maintenance or underfunding reserves. The only way to know is to examine appropriate documents.

 Bottom line: *Do not depend on the level of association assessments to determine the financial health of the association.*

Myth #7: The condo is in a nice area of town, so it must be well built and operating well with no problems.

I have worked with associations in many different neighborhoods, and location is generally not a factor in determining if the association is in good health. A low-rise complex in a working-class neighborhood could be in much better financial shape than a high-rise complex in a trendy area of town. Due diligence is required.

 Bottom line: *Do not be swayed by the area of town in which the condominium resides. Condominium surprises come from all areas of town.*

Myth #8: The lender has approved the deal, so the lender must believe there are no hidden surprises.

Lenders are doing a much better job of considering the financial health of associations. However, they are not in a position of performing the due diligence that is outlined in this book. In fact, most lenders only require that 10 percent of total assessments be contributed to reserves. This is further explained in myth #9.

Bottom line: *Do not depend on lenders to analyze the financial health of the association.*

Myth #9: I am using an FHA loan to acquire the condo, which means the association needs to be approved by HUD (United States Department of Housing and Urban Development); therefore, there should be no surprises.

Condominium associations now need to be approved and certified by HUD to allow purchasers to use FHA loan products. FHA loans allow the purchaser to put less money down; qualifying ratios are more liberal and represent a large share of all loans written for condominiums. HUD requires condominium associations to adhere to a strict set of criteria regarding insurance, rental unit maximums, and federal policies. However, HUD changed the requirement for associations to fully fund reserves several years ago.

Currently, to qualify for HUD certification, a condominium association merely needs to contribute 10 percent of the total monthly condominium assessment to reserves. At first glance, this may sound like an adequate amount. However, most associations need to be contributing at least one-third of the total assessments to the reserve fund to adequately pay for future repairs and replacements, including replacing the roof, painting, siding, windows, doors, et cetera. If a condominium association does not contribute enough money to the reserve fund, a special assessment will likely follow in the year funds are needed. The fact that a condominium association is HUD certified does not guarantee that the association has adequately funded reserves to avoid a future special assessment.

Bottom line: *Do not depend on government agencies such as HUD to analyze the financial health of the association.*

Myth #10: My state has numerous state statutes designed to protect condominium owners, so there should be no surprises.

Many states have statutes designed to protect buyers and current owners of condominium associations. These statutes, which vary from state to state, may include the requirement of reviewed or audited financial statements, prepared reserve studies, and laws that give members certain rights with respect to living within an association. However, very few states have the ability to monitor whether associations are complying with statutes, and very few have any fines relating to noncompliance. Even if your state has statutes designed to protect buyers and existing members, you still need to determine that the association is in compliance. In reality, this may not be an effective safeguard.

Bottom line: *Do not depend on state statutes to safeguard you from financial harm.*

Myth #11: The association has over $200,000 in the reserve bank account, so it looks like the association is in good shape.

Depending on the association, $200,000 may be a grossly underfunded reserve fund, and the association may be headed for a special assessment. The only way to determine if the reserve fund is adequately funded is to analyze the reserve study discussed in chapter 16.

Bottom line: *Do not depend on the bank balance of the association; it may be grossly inadequate.*

Myth #12: The developer has been in business for a long time and has built many communities in my area, so the condo I am buying is probably well built with no surprises.

Developers can have good projects and bad projects. Much depends on the subcontractors and oversight of the project. When business is booming, many condominium projects are built, contractors are hard to find, and work is performed as fast as possible to get the units on the market quickly. Some developers consistently build great projects. However, relying on reputation alone can be a problem. Due diligence should still be performed on every potential purchase.

Bottom line: *Do not depend on the reputation of the developer. Due diligence includes performing all procedures outlined in this book.*

Myth #13: The association is managed by a big property management company, so everything must be going well with the association.

Management companies can only do so much with a board and membership that chooses not to pay attention to sound financial management and common sense. Good management companies can help boards fulfill their fiduciary duties, but buyers still need to perform due diligence and expand their analysis to appropriate procedures outlined in the book.

Bottom line: *Do not depend on the reputation of the management company.*

Myth #14: The condominium was built in the 1970s, so if anything bad was going to happen to the property, it would have happened by now.

Projects built in the 1970s have issues that are different than newer condominiums. Components such as plumbing, water/sewer lines, windows, siding, and other long-lived assets are nearing the end of their estimated useful lives. Many reserve studies do not have these components listed; thus, the association may not have saved for their eventual replacement. The age of the condominium may be a potential red flag unless proper inspections have been performed and the reserve study is adequate.

Bottom line: *The age of the condominium may matter greatly.*

Myth #15: The other members of the condominium are mostly professional types, so everyone will likely be very reasonable. No surprises.

I have worked with thousands of white-collar, blue-collar, and no-collar associations over the past thirty years. A person's professional and educational background does not guarantee that the financial affairs of the association are in order. Due diligence is still required.

Bottom line: *Do not depend on the appearance of association members.*

Myth #16: My condominium was just built, so I shouldn't expect any surprises.

New condominiums pose a different set of potential issues. Construction defects, developers not properly funding reserves, and developers who subsidize the monthly association fees until the project is substantially sold out are issues unique to new projects. Due diligence should still be performed.

Bottom line: *Do not depend on the fact that the condominium is newly constructed.*

Myth #17: I was told the condominium assessments have not increased in the last ten years, so I don't have to worry about an in increase in fees or a special assessment. (Included in this is favoring a condominium that has the lowest fees of any condominium on the market.)

This is a major red flag! Associations that have not raised assessments over the years may not be funding reserves properly or not providing adequate maintenance to building components. This greatly increases the chance of a special assessment. Due diligence in the form of additional analysis is required.

Bottom line: *Do not depend on past assessment increases.*

Myth #18: The association is audited by an independent certified public accountant, so everything must be in order.

Certainly the involvement of a CPA who understands associations will help bring issues to the attention of the board. However, audits happen generally three to nine months after the close of a year and may not give the purchaser the most up-to-date information. They also do not give an opinion on the adequacy of reserves. Due diligence in the form of additional analysis is required.

Bottom line: *Do not depend solely on the work of a CPA to base a decision.*

Myth #19: The association has a reserve study.

A reserve study prepared by a credentialed provider can help associations determine how much money to save to pay for future repairs and maintenance on common area property. However, there are different levels of reserve studies. The information in the study may not be accurate, and the study may not be supported by a complete building envelope inspection. Also, the association may not be following the recommended contribution to the reserve bank account.

Bottom line: *A reserve study may give the buyer limited assurance, but due diligence is required to determine how much assurance can be placed on the study and whether the association is following the recommended contribution to reserves.*

Myth #20: I have obtained a disclosure certificate from the seller that should tell me about all issues I need to be concerned about.

A disclosure certificate is a statement given to the potential buyer by the seller. It includes information that may alert the buyer of potential concerns. This certificate may save you time in gathering needed information relating to the financial condition of the association, including construction defects and litigation, but it should not be the sole determining source of investigation.

Bottom line: *A disclosure certificate may help in providing needed information, but due diligence is still required to analyze this information and to gather information not included in the disclosure certificate to make a well-informed decision.*

Chapter Takeaways

Every mention of due diligence throughout this chapter can be read as this chapter's main takeaway: this chapter is meant to perk up your ears and entice you to sit up a little straighter in your seat as you move further into concepts explored in the chapters to come. This—for a reader, a buyer, an owner, a board member, or a person in a combination of these roles—is part of your due diligence.

4

The Legal Foundation

It is important for buyers, sellers, and members to have a basic understanding of the legal foundation of associations. Over the last thirty years of consulting with association community managers, boards, and members, I have found that many answers to questions can be located in the governing documents that compose the legal framework of the association. In addition, state statutes and federal laws and regulations also govern the affairs of the association and may affect a decision to buy or stay in an association.

There are four basic characteristics of most associations:

1. All owners are automatically members of a community association.
2. Governing documents create mutual obligations.
3. Mandatory fees or assessment are levied against owners for operations and maintenance.
4. All owners share a property interest in the community.

Planned communities (PUDs) and condominiums differ in certain unique aspects. Planned communities generally consist of single-family homes or, in some communities, townhomes. Planned community homeowners associations generally own common area property such as common area land, clubhouses, and tennis courts, while each member owns his or her home and the land under the home, which is deeded to the member. The distinguishing characteristic of planned communities is that each member is responsible for all maintenance and replacement of his or her home, including the interior and exterior components. Townhome owners within a planned community could either be responsible for all interior and exterior components or, depending on how the documents are written, be responsible only for the interior components, and the association could be responsible for exterior components such as roofs, siding, windows, and painting.

Condominiums, which are generally multistory buildings with units built on top of one another, are usually platted differently. The member of a condominium owns and is responsible for the interior of the unit, which in many cases begins with the middle of the wall and moves inward. Attics may or may not be the responsibility of the member, depending on how the documents are written. The exterior components in a condominium (the middle of the wall and outward) are generally the responsibility of the association. This may include the roof, gutters, windows, doors, decks, siding, painting, asphalt, cement walkways, curbs, and other exterior components.

It should be noted that sometimes even attorneys find it difficult while reviewing association documents to determine if the association is filed as a condominium or as a planned community. Why is this important? Certain states have different state statutes for planned communities and condominiums. You would think that since the operation and obligations of both types of associations are basically the same after determining which party is responsible for certain components, the state statutes would be the same for condominiums and planned communities. However, this is not always the case, and care should be taken to determine the correct filing status in order to reference the correct and applicable state statute. The CC&Rs (*Covenants, Conditions, and Restrictions* discussed in chapter 2) may or may not indicate whether the member or the association is responsible for windows, doors, and decks. Care should be taken to understand the repair and replacement responsibilities of the member and of the association to ensure proper funding at the association level. It may be advisable to engage an attorney to assist in this determination.

To further compound these issues is the fact that in some cases townhomes may be platted and filed as a planned community, yet the CC&Rs require the association to maintain, repair, and replace all exterior components much the same as they would a condominium. In rare instances, townhomes may be platted as a planned community, with each owner responsible for all interior and exterior components such as roofs, siding, painting, windows, and doors. The dividing line of responsibility is the middle of the wall that adjoins each townhome. An unsuspecting buyer may initially think that this type of community is better since the homeowner dues are much lower because the association does not have to save for future repairs and replacements of common area components relating to the units. However, what happens when it is time to paint, and some owners want to paint and others do not? What about paint colors? It is possible to have the CC&Rs spell out these issues, thus avoiding conflict and drama. However, it is my opinion that such communities should be viewed critically, with greater attention paid to these issues.

The importance of these issues relate to who is ultimately responsible for the maintenance, repair, replacement, and insurance responsibilities of components. I have witnessed instances when older associations have never legally determined the maintenance, repair, and replacement responsibilities of components such as windows, doors, and decks because the CC&Rs were silent about such components or unclear as to ultimate responsibility. A buyer would need to know this before scheduling the inspection of the unit to ensure applicable components are included in the inspection report and considered when evaluating the purchase.

The ownership of the common components is what drives the association dues charged to the members. These fees include amounts for operating expenses as well as assessments to save for future repairs and replacements of common area property. Association fees are calculated based on the provisions of the CC&Rs. There are two methods used to allocate association expenses to members. One way is to have each member pay the same amount of assessments monthly. This method works well for condominiums that are very similar in size and complexity for each unit. This is also the prevalent method for planned communities. Another method uses the square footage of each condominium unit in relation to the square footage of all units as a way of allocating the assessment. Thus, larger condominiums pay more than smaller units in terms of square footage.

As discussed in chapters 8 and 10, associations are governed not only by the CC&RS but also by federal, state, and local laws as well as rules and regulations adopted by an association's board. The order in which associations must comply with the aforementioned statutes and regulations is as follows: federal, state, local, CC&Rs, and board rules and regulations. Thus, federal laws trump the CC&Rs if there are conflicting requirements.

Board members have a fiduciary duty to follow all provisions of federal, state, and local laws; CC&Rs; and rules and regulations adopted by the board. Board members do not always follow such requirements, thus causing disharmony within the association.

Willful neglect of the aforementioned provisions may cause board members to be at risk of negating directors' and officers' insurance coverage. Traditionally, legal action is not consummated where negligence of current and ex–board members is concerned.

However, current and ex–board members may be at risk for claims of negligence. Boards may also find that the directors' and officers' insurance coverage may not cover directors if boards are found to be in willful neglect of provisions. Not following these provisions may also create a culture of noncompliance.

Chapter Takeaways

- The legal framework of the association may have an impact on your purchase.
- There are four basic characteristics to most associations: all owners are automatically members of a community association; governing documents create mutual obligations; mandatory fees or assessments are levied against owners for operations and maintenance; and all owners share a property interest in the community.
- Boards should always follow all provisions of federal, state, and local laws and regulations as well as the CC&Rs.

Tips—Best Practices

- Board members, community managers, and owners should be well versed in the legal requirements and attributes of the association.
- An association should have its legal documents reviewed periodically by an attorney specializing in homeowners associations. This review should include updating the documents to include changes in federal, state, and local statutes in order to clear up

any ambiguities in the provisions. *Be particularly wary of a board that drafts its own regulations without consulting an attorney.*

- Only experienced HOA attorneys should amend documents or draft important resolutions.
- **Buyers:** Be aware of the importance of federal, state, and local laws and statutes documents, as well as documents such as the CC&Rs. These documents are mentioned throughout the book with special emphasis on particular issues affecting buyers, sellers, and members.

Tips—Creating Community

If all parties are following the provisions of the legal documents, there will be less drama all around, which will in turn allow for increased harmony among the members. Following the rules pays off for everyone involved!

Further Reading

- Local, state, and federal statutes regarding associations and the governing documents for the association that is being considered or the association with which you have a membership
- *The Homeowners Association Manual*, Peter M. Dunbar, Esq., and Marc W. Dunbar, Esq.[1]
- *The Law of Condominium Operations*, by Gary A. Poliakoff[2]
- *Community Association Law: Cases and Materials on Common Interest Communities*, second edition, by Wayne S. Hyatt and Susan F. French[3]
- *The Condominium Concept: A Practical Guide for Officers, Owners, Realtors, Attorneys, and Directors of Florida Condominiums*, thirteenth edition, by Peter M. Dunbar, Esq.[4]

5

Condominiums and PUDs—
Formation and Operations

At this juncture, I explore the differences in home ownership between condominiums and other housing options within an association. For the purposes of this chapter, I examine condominiums and planned unit developments (or PUDs). For information on timeshares and cooperatives, please see the discussions in chapters 22 and 23, respectively.

There are two distinct forms of home ownership: planned unit developments and condominiums. Condominiums and PUDs are often referred to as community associations, common ownership communities, or homeowners associations—all of those terms refer to ownership of buildings and land. It is *how* one owns that differs.

Perhaps the most significant difference is how land is owned. In a PUD, the owner owns an individual plot of land upon which the home sits. As realtors sometimes put it, the owner owns to the depths of the earth and to the reaches of the sky. The owner may have a freestanding, single-family home or may own part of a building that shares common walls—usually called a townhome or a row house. In either instance, that person is a lot owner, owning the building and the land underneath it. The home sits on an identified tax lot, and the owner pays taxes individually on the home and land.

A condominium most often is thought of as a multistory building with one or more units on each floor. However, a condominium can also be in a row house or townhome style. The distinguishing characteristic of all condominiums is that one sits on one single lot, and ownership of that lot is shared in an undivided interest—that is, each owner shares in the ownership of the entire parcel. The unit owner is taxed on the value of the unit. Associations generally do not pay property taxes on land under the units or on common area property. Taxing authorities include the value of the land, including common area property, in the value of the unit when assessing property taxes, and the association is taxed on the value of the land. The value of the common area is deemed to be an integral part of the value of the unit or home and is taxed at the individual-owner level.

Fee Simple/Leasehold Ownership

Most property owned within an association is owned "fee simple"— the owner has an absolute interest in the property either individually or pro rata with other members. In some areas, such as Hawaii, condominium associations lease the land under the structure as well as adjoining common area property. These are generally long-term leases that expire years in the future. However, an older project may be getting close to the end of the property lease. Lenders are keenly aware of this and often do not extend payment terms beyond the date of lease expiration.

From a buyer standpoint, this should be taken into consideration because at the end of lease the owner of the land would most likely want to renegotiate the lease terms and increase the monthly or yearly fee or, in the worst case, cancel the lease.

General Common Elements and Limited Common Elements

How much a unit owner in a condominium owns individually is set forth in the governing documents. Anything in the walls, such as wires, plumbing, and HVAC pipes, is generally owned in common, no matter that a specific wire or pipe may be delivering directly to a specific unit.

The building and the land on which the unit stands are referred to as general common elements. This includes the roof, siding, common hallways and entrances, sidewalks and possibly parking areas, and common facilities. Also included are the structural elements of the building, such as the foundation and load bearing walls, common HVAC, landscaped areas, and anything that is used by all owners.

Additionally, a condominium may have limited common elements. These are parts of the condominium that are set forth for the exclusive use of one or more owners but not all. Examples include decks, patios, and parking spaces and could include an elevator that only services one or more of the top floors. Depending on the documents, the association may be responsible for repairs, maintenance, and replacement of limited common elements, or the owners who have exclusive use may be responsible.

Development and Governance

Both condominiums and PUDs have declarations and bylaws (CC&Rs), and each has a board of directors elected by the owners to manage the association. While the declaration and bylaws of a PUD townhome usually gives the exterior building maintenance to the association, an owner of a PUD townhome may have more responsibility for maintenance than an individual in a condominium. As always, the documents set out the responsibilities of both the owner and the association.

Many associations are organized as nonprofit entities. An association is initially formed when the declarant (developer) files the necessary paperwork with the applicable state jurisdiction. Once the project obtains the certificate of occupancy allowing buyers to legally purchase the unit, the declarant files the documents with the county, including but not limited to the CC&Rs and disclosure statements and, if required, initial budgets.

The documents filed set up the structure of the association and the rules governing it. The developer then sets up a budget and the basic administrative procedures and is responsible for maintaining a record and minutes of board and association meetings as well as any related documents.

As the development of the property progresses, the board will be made up of the developer's representatives. There is often a larger number of votes per unit belonging to the developer than to new owners. Normally the architectural committee is made up of the developer's representatives. In other words, the developer maintains total control until a *turnover* occurs (see definition in chapter 2). Turnover is the point when the owners have a meeting to elect their own board members.

The developer obviously wants to protect the investment, and rules normally are spelled out in the documents giving that protection. However, the developer also owes a fiduciary duty to owners, so the developer does not have a right to act contrary to the legitimate interests of the owners. A wise developer starts with the first buyer, educating each person as to the new owners' responsibilities and rights.

During the phase of declarant control, the developer wears at least two hats: as a member of the association and as the developer in charge of sales and turning a profit on the project. I have seen instances where the developer charged the association sales costs or interior maintenance costs even though these costs are the responsibility of the developer. In some instances, the developer comingled accounting of the association with the activities of the developer. It became difficult to ascertain which entity was paying for the correct expenses.

During the developer phase, the documents may provide for an advisory board of owners after a certain amount of sales. The advisory board does not have authority over the association, but it can and should be a conduit for communications between the developer and the owners and can serve as a training format for future board members. While the developer maintains decision control, the advisory board may be able to provide the owners with a format for input on decisions that need to be made before turnover.

Turnover

As mentioned above, turnover is the point when control by the developer, through the chosen board, is turned over to the owners. Normally there is a meeting of owners, at which they elect the board members to run the association's business. In some circumstances, the developer may have the right to have a member on the board. In such circumstances, that membership will end when either the last home is sold or a certain percentage is reached.

At turnover, all documents should be turned over to the new board. It is also very helpful if the board can receive a schedule of the expected life of materials, copies of warranties, a list of manufacturers, building and landscape plans, as well as "as builts" (a revised set of drawings submitted by the contractor or contractors showing all changes made during construction) and approvals from any appropriate government entities (for example, confirmation that fire hydrants are placed according to the local governmental plan). Also important are copies of all contracts signed by the developer on behalf of the association (such as landscape maintenance) and a list with contact info for the general contractor (if different from the developer) and all subcontractors.

Role of the Developer

In summary, a developer (referred to as the declarant in legal documents) creates the association by filing documents with the state under specific state laws. The developer then builds the condominium or single-home development and readies the property for sale. The activity of the association commences upon the sale of the first unit or home.

The developer is generally in full control of the association in the early operations of the association. This may present a conflict of interest for the developer since the developer is concerned with keeping dues low to spur sales and may not address certain construction defect issues. Even though the developer has certain fiduciary duties to act in the best interest of the association, this is sometimes not the case through willful neglect or incompetence.

Role of the Owners

Owners elect the board members (and usually have authority to remove them). In some states, owners have a right to approve or reject a new budget. Normally, only owners may be elected to the board. Owners also have the power to amend the declaration and particular sections of the bylaws, such as those dealing with assessments and sale of common property. The documents set out the required percentage of votes required to make such changes.

Along with those rights come obligations that are set out in the CC&Rs. These are binding obligations and can be enforced by a court. Among them is the obligation to pay assessments on time. Occasionally, a case makes it to court where an owner is withholding payment of assessments pending resolution of a different dispute with the board. In general, those cases are decided against the owner.

The association often has the power to put a lien* on the property. While most owners never have to deal with liens, owners should be aware that a lien could result in the loss of the home.

Although there is no legal obligation to actively participate in the association, failure to participate leaves decisions to those who are willing. Community spirit is not legislated but goes very far toward making the association a pleasant and rewarding place to live—rewarding in that a community with a positive outlook is one that actively maintains property values.

Role of the Board

The board manages the community. The authority to act is set out in the governing documents and sometimes by state or federal law or case law and, thus, is not unlimited. Boards have the authority to set goals, standards, and policies and to enforce them and the governing documents; to maintain property, provide insurance, and collect assessments; and to enter into contracts, create and supervise committees, and conduct annual meetings and board meetings. Some states will grant broad authority such as corporations have; other states may be very precise as to the board's power and duties.

---

*A lien is a legal procedure that places a hold on selling the property until the debt owed to the association is paid.

An example of a specific state rule is a California law permitting an association to relocate residents when tenting for termites. Some laws and documents may not only permit but require certain actions, such as providing adequate insurance or distributing financial statements to owners. Some prohibit certain decisions. For example, courts have found that a board acted without authority in one case when the board sold property without following procedures in the documents; in another case, a board failed to obtain owners' consent before exercising a right of first refusal.

Federal law occasionally impacts board decisions. The federal Fair Housing Act of 1988 states, among other things, that an association may not discriminate based on familial status or handicap. Based on the Fair Housing Act, a Florida court prohibited an association from enforcing two rules, one that prohibited children from using a pool except between 11:00 AM and 2:00 PM, and the other that prohibited children under five from using the pool.*

If a board acts without authority, fails to act when required, or acts when prohibited, courts may find the act invalid and the board members liable. The court may find that the board must pay the judgment out of their own pockets, and that insurance protecting board members does not apply.

Role of the Officers

Typically, a board has four officers: president, vice president, treasurer, and secretary.

The president chairs meetings, signs contracts on behalf of the corporation, and may have the right to select or nominate committee chairs.

---

*This is possible except in the case of a community with age qualifications, such as a retirement community.

The vice president acts in the place of the president when the president is not available and shares in the general duties. Often the vice president is assigned as the liaison to certain committees.

The treasurer works with various parties to ensure that the budget proposal for the next year is developed and that all financial records, including a roster of delinquent accounts, is kept. The treasurer recommends actions to be taken for collections and receipt and disbursement of funds and is responsible for periodic financial reports and any independent financial review or audit. If there is a manager, the manager may be tasked with much of this work, but ultimately the treasurer is responsible. Details on the responsibilities and tasks associated with the treasurer's position can be found in appendix A, section 1.

The secretary is responsible for ensuring the meeting agendas are properly prepared and distributed, notices are given, and minutes are properly taken, and the secretary maintains all official records, including official correspondence, contracts, and the membership roster. (An example board meeting agenda and minutes can be found in appendix F). While some of this may be delegated to a manager, the secretary is ultimately responsible for these tasks and may need to sign official documents along with the president.

Role of the Committees

The documents, and particularly the bylaws, may identify certain committees or authorize the board to appoint committees. Committees serve three purposes: they assist the board by gathering information and making recommendations; they broaden the community's input by gathering residents' opinions; and they serve as a training ground for new board members.

One of the most consistent committees is the architectural committee. Other committees include maintenance, elections or nominating, budget and finance, rule enforcement, newsletter, social or recreation, risk management, and landscaping.

The board should clearly delineate, preferably by resolution, each committee's authority and scope or responsibility, membership, term of office, and relationship of the committee to the board.

If the board has committees, it should ensure that the committees have meaningful tasks and adequate authority to complete them. When committees make recommendations, the board should give serious consideration to the result.

In most, if not all situations, the board is ultimately responsible for any decision. While authority might be given to a committee to make a decision, the board should be aware of decisions being made. Because committees may sometimes address an issue that is outside the scope of authority in the documents, it is the duty of the board to make sure that ultimately the documents are followed. For example, an architectural committee may have specific authority from the documents over design issues. That does not extend the authority to rule over engineering issues.

If a committee has authority to make decisions, there should be a clear process for an owner to appeal a decision. In some circumstances, that may be an appeal directly to the full board or to a subset of the board or hearing committee, which then makes a recommendation to the full board.

Chapter Takeaways

- **Buyers:** Understanding the difference between a PUD and a condominium may be helpful in analyzing information and documents you will encounter.
- Many of the issues discussed in this book pertain to *both* condominium developments and single-family home developments within an association. Keep this in mind as you move forward.

- Understanding the different roles played by the board, manager, committees, and so on can help in determining who to contact. This may be particularly helpful for members selling their units or homes since the authority for requesting information resides with a member of the association. Read more about governance in chapter 10.

Tips—Best Practices

- An association that has well-documented policies, procedures, and an operating manual detailing all the aspects of management tends to operate smoothly with decreased chance of surprises.
- Boards and community managers should be well versed in the operations and specifics of their association.

Tips—Creating Community

- Knowledgeable boards and members can greatly help the operations of the community.
- Well-informed boards and community managers can use best practices discussed in this book to create a harmonious lifestyle for all members.

Further Reading

New Neighborhoods: The Consumer's Guide to Condominium, Co-op, and HOA Living, by Gary A. Poliakoff and Ryan Poliakoff[1]

6
Management vs. Self-Management

There are no hard-and-fast rules as to whether or not a condominium should be self-managed or managed by a professional management company. There are condominium communities that have been very successfully self-managed for years. As with most things, there are trade-offs. Even if the association has a manager, the ultimate responsibility for the maintenance and operation of the condominium resides with the board of directors.

With larger associations, there is potentially a larger pool of people who may have backgrounds that would benefit the board and committees. Small associations too often make the decision regarding management assistance based on perceived costs, not realizing that each choice—to hire or go it alone—has its own unique costs and benefits.

A self-managed board must educate itself on some difficult-to-understand association-governing documents. Through trial and error, board members need to build a list of reliable contractors. Someone has to keep the books. There has to be someone who will handle emergencies, and all of this work must be done in the owners' free time. So the reasoning that self-managing will "save money" may or may not be a realistic evaluation in terms of needs being met. Self-management has physical, emotional, and financial costs, particularly if the board and committees make errors that will bring liability to the association.

Prospective buyers of condominiums have an expectation of maintenance-free living but often don't realize this comes because of the involvement of the owners of that condominium. With self-management, that involvement is going to be significantly higher.

With a self-managed condominium, there may be a higher sense of community and a more palpable pride of ownership, as people tend to be more aware that they are responsible for the maintenance needed. Arguably, people are more passionate and committed to their association. And it stands to reason that if a prospective buyer is considering a self-managed association, that person will be asked to volunteer to help carry the load.

On the other hand, self-management may be a sign that owners fail to understand both the requirements of the governing documents and the limitations of authority they may contain. This inevitably leads to problems in the management of the community and results in problems that may be far more costly than what a manager might have cost.

Chapter Takeaways

Self-managed associations may be an effective method of managing the affairs of the association. However, to be effective, the association operations should be well documented to allow for the transition of board members and officers. **Buyers:** Be aware that being self-managed could be a red flag.

Tips—Best Practices

Associations should have all policies, procedures, and operations documented in a procedures manual approved by the board. Such policies and procedures should not be changed without careful consideration and approval by the board.

Tips—Creating Community

Consistency in operations with well-thought-out policies and procedures can help ensure a financially viable association and good quality of life for the members.

Further Reading

- *Self-Management: A Guide for the Small Community Association,* second edition, by Debra H. Lewin and Ellen De Haan[1]
- *GAP Report: Choosing a Management Company,* fifth edition, by Michael E. Packard[2]

7

Covenants, Conditions, and Restrictions (CC&Rs) and Local, State, and Federal Statutes

CC&Rs

As touched on in previous chapters, CC&Rs contain two documents. First, the declaration, which includes but is not limited to describing the boundaries of the units, disclosure provisions, restrictions on the use of the property, enforcement powers, assessments, obligations, and lien/collection rights, duty to insure, dispute resolution and attorneys' fees provisions, member rights, rental restrictions, occupancy restrictions, mold liability, insurance provisions, and maintenance and repair responsibilities.

Second, the bylaws include but are not limited to the manner in which the association is to be governed. These provisions include cumulative voting, quorum requirements, director qualifications including terms of office, nomination of directors and election procedures, budgets and requirements of a reserve for future replacements and the preparation of a reserve study, due process requirements, records inspection, duties of officers, et cetera.

Certain provisions could be located in either document, depending on the manner in which the documents are written.

CC&R restrictions may include landscaping guidelines, including types of trees or bushes and grass height; house color, including trim; size and types of outbuildings like sheds and garages; pets, including types and sizes (for example, only cats and dogs under twenty pounds); outdoor decorations (both year-round and holiday); signs; parking; and the definition of junk as it applies to items visible in your yard, including cars on blocks and gardening tools or unattractive benches.

Please be aware that these documents are deeded to your property. When you purchase your unit or house, you are deemed to understand these documents and have agreed to abide by them.

Associations are obligated to enforce these provisions and will take all necessary steps for enforcement, including fines and legal action.

Please also understand that if you rent your unit or house, your tenants will be obligated to obey these provisions. If they do not, you may be fined.

If, after reading these documents, you find a provision that you cannot live with, such as not being able to have a pet over twenty pounds, please do not think you can simply enact a change in the documents once you become a member. The CC&Rs can be very difficult to change (amend). The documents can require anywhere between a 67 percent and a 90 percent affirmative vote of the membership to amend. It is sometimes very difficult to get this type of affirmative vote even on very popular changes.

At times, there are provisions in the CC&Rs that may restrict a legitimate right. For example, restrictions on pets may, on a specific reading, prevent an owner from having a service dog. While service dogs are recognized under the Americans with Disabilities Act (ADA), there are numerous examples of lawsuits to enforce this right. There are also lawsuits brought against associations concerning such things as flying the US flag and free speech issues concerning signs. And not all lawsuits brought concerning these matters are concluded in the owner's favor.

Local, State, and Federal Statutes

State statutes are laws enacted by each state that relate to the formation and governance of the association. Each state adopts its own laws. CC&Rs should adhere to state statutes and adopt these provisions in the documents of the association. Local statutes are different for each municipality and should be investigated if appropriate.

State statutes, federal statutes, and the CC&Rs are the most relevant. State statutes take precedence over CC&Rs, and it should also be noted that federal laws take precedence over state statutes and CC&Rs. Examples are fair housing laws that regulate discrimination and other matters.

Keep in mind that, depending on when statutes were approved and when the documents of each association were written, the documents may not agree to current statutes. Many associations do not want to incur the cost of updating their CC&Rs. This can lead to confusion within the association. Care should be taken to ensure that no existing provisions restrict your ability to have a pleasurable experience within the association.

Chapter Takeaways

- Read the CC&Rs (declaration and bylaws) very carefully. **Buyers:** You may find provisions in them that you are not willing to accept.
- CC&Rs are enforceable and are difficult to amend. Make sure there are no provisions that would affect your quality of life within the association before buying.
- Federal laws and then state statutes take precedence over CC&Rs.

Tips—Best Practices

Adherence to all CC&Rs, as well as federal, state, and local laws and regulations, helps ensure that boards meet their fiduciary responsibilities.

Tips—Creating Community

CC&Rs and applicable statutes provide a framework for governing that can create stability within the community. When members believe that the board of directors adheres to a set of rules for governance, this can set the stage for a harmonious community.

Further Reading

- "Corporation and Security Law: State and Federal Regulation of Condominiums," *Marquette Law Review*, by David J. Minahan[1]
- "Condominium Homeownership in the United States: A Selected Annotated Bibliography of Legal Sources," *Law Library Journal*, by Donna S. Bennett[2]

8

Rules and Regulations

Rules and regulations of the association are different from the governing documents (CC&Rs) and state statutes in that they are not laws of the state or deeded into the documents. However, they can have the same authority if properly written, voted on by the board of directors, and administered consistently.

Rules and regulations can be as simple as rules relating to the swimming pool or as far-reaching as restricting the size of a pet. They may also include parking restrictions and the type of vehicle allowed in the parking lot. Rules generally cover the "three p's": pets, people, and parking. Rules frequently cover:

- Landscaping
    - Conditions for unit owner plantings
    - Guidelines for unit owner plantings
    - Grade
- Motor vehicles
- Pets

- Exterior modifications
  - Additions, alterations, improvements
  - Storm/screen doors and storm windows
  - Paint
  - Front door hardware
  - Patios and decks
- Use of common areas
- Miscellaneous
  - Annoyance
  - Outside attachment to buildings
  - Signs: For Sale, For Rent, and other
  - Combustible materials
  - Seasonal decorations
  - Smoke detectors
  - Garbage disposals
  - Enforcement of rules and regulations

Associations often post rules and regulations online or send the rules out to the membership periodically. However, many associations do not notify new members of the current rules and regulations. By the time owners buy their units and find out about a rule that may affect them, it is too late.

Worst-case scenario: You buy a condominium and do not ask for the rules and regulations before you buy. The rules and regulations state that no dogs over thirty-five pounds are allowed in the common areas. You buy your unit, and one of your neighbors reports that your fifty-pound collie is over the weight limit. The board of directors writes you a letter reminding you of the rule. You write back and inform the board that you were not told of this rule when buying your unit. The board writes back and informs you that it was your responsibility to inquire about rules before buying your unit. You write back and request an exception to the rule. The board writes back and states there are no exceptions. The board also informs you that beginning on a specific date you will be fined $10 a day until your dog is off the premises.

Some of the details may be more nuanced than this example, but the general point stands: you may be faced with daily fines or losing your pet altogether because you did not request and read the rules and regulations before buying.

There may be many rules and regulations that impact your quality of life within the association. State statutes are a matter of law, and governing documents are deeded into your unit, making it relatively easy to obtain these documents. Rules and regulations, on the other hand, may not be readily available. Care should be taken to make sure you have all rules and regulations before buying. The fact that no one provided you with the rules and regulations when buying even after you asked for them may not be a defense if confronted with actions of the board of directors. Also consider that rules and regulations may change from time to time at the discretion of the board of directors.

Chapter Takeaways

Obtain a list of rules and regulations and be aware of typical rules and regulations that may affect your quality of life.

Tips—Best Practices

Associations should strive to adopt reasonable rules and regulations and provide them to the membership.

Tips—Creating Community

Members should have input into the rules-and-regulations process.

9

Minutes

Minutes are notes taken at board meetings and committee meetings of the association. Minutes document, among other things, actions taken by the board of directors or, in the case of a committee, actions proposed to the board for deliberation and vote. The minutes can be a wealth of information to a prospective buyer. Minutes may include a discussion or action on the following issues:

- A potential special assessment
- Construction defects
- Assessment delinquencies, which may require an increase in dues
- Budget considerations
- Shortfalls in cash
- Potential or existing litigation
- Infighting among the board and/or members
- Proposed rules

- Crime and vandalism statistics
- Foreclosures

There are different types of board meetings and related minutes. They include but are not limited to the following:

- Regular board meetings
- Emergency meetings
- Annual meetings
- Executive session meetings
- Committee meetings

Associations are typically required to hold a certain number of board meetings during the year to conduct the business of the association. The secretary of the association is required to record minutes of the association meeting. Association attorneys are quick to point out that minutes of the association should be concise and not include verbiage relating to discussions, comments, and other proceedings of the board meeting. However, it is my experience that minutes do contain a lot of information other than the resolution to be voted on and whether the motion passes or fails. It is precisely from this extra information that we can learn a lot about the association. My firm, in reviewing the minutes of one of our financial statement clients, noted an interaction between one of the members and the board of directors in which the member promptly turned his back on the board, lowered his trousers, and mooned the board. This type of information is not pertinent to finances or regulations but does show other indications of a board's health, or lack of it.

Minutes are taken not only during regular board meetings but also during committee meetings. Finance, architectural, and building and grounds committee meetings can also offer a wealth of information regarding association governance. When asking for minutes, ask for all committee as well as regular meeting minutes.

Minutes are obtained from the property management firm or board secretary, if self-managed. The seller of the unit may have to request copies of the minutes. Be prepared to pay for copying costs and handling fees. If you are told there are no minutes of board meetings, this would be a red flag. It is doubtful that the association is being governed in accordance with the CC&Rs.

It is not unusual for a board president to call an executive session meeting during a regular board meeting. Executive sessions are called to discuss matters that the board believes should not be discussed during an open board meeting with members of the association. Subject matters discussed in executive sessions typically include salary and employee issues, vendor contracts, and potential and existing litigation.

Minutes of executive sessions are not taken; therefore, it may not be possible to obtain information about these sessions. However, when the executive session ends and the regular meeting of the board of directors reconvenes, a motion is made to confirm decisions made in the executive session. There may also be verbiage in the regular board meeting minutes that can give you information about matters discussed in executive sessions—most concerning would be litigation issues.

Key words to pay attention to when reviewing minutes are:

- Special assessment
- Litigation
- Operating budget shortfall
- Construction defects
- Underfunding reserves
- Borrowing from reserves
- Borrowing from bank
- Drama among members

- Potential rule enactment
- Past-due assessments
- Repair and replacement projects over budget

Chapter Takeaways

- Minutes are the official record of recommendations or decisions made at committee and board meetings.
- Minutes can alert a buyer to potential issues that may have a financial impact after purchase.
- Lack of minutes of a committee or board meeting is a sign of poor governance.

Tips—Best Practices

Minutes should capture all motions and the outcome of the vote. They should not include extraneous comments and verbiage.

Tips—Creating Community

Minutes should be made available to all members to ensure the members are kept abreast of all issues.

Further Reading

"How to Take Minutes," WikiHow[1]

10

Governance

An association is governed by a board of directors appointed by the declarant before the turnover or elected by membership after the turnover occurs. The board is elected by the membership. The powers of the board are documented in the CC&Rs and state statutes. Officers are then elected by the board. As noted previously, these positions include president (or chairman), vice president (or vice chairman), secretary, and treasurer. The background of board members can vary widely.

It should be noted that serving on the board is at times a thankless and demanding job. Therefore, it is sometimes very difficult to find qualified people to serve on the board. As a result, the qualifications to fill a board position are at times not based on the most qualified candidate, rather, the most available candidate. All associations are different with respect to the quality of board governance. Certainly, an experienced property management firm can assist in guiding the board, but the board makes the final decision on association matters. You should not assume the board is following provisions of the CC&Rs, state statutes, or association rules and regulations or making decisions in the best interests of the association as a whole.

Although state statutes governing associations vary from state to state, there are basic tenants of governance embodied in the governing documents and rules and regulations. These provisions may include but are not limited to:

- Holding meetings of the board of directors
- Recording minutes of meetings of the board of directors
- Adopting an annual budget
- Adopting a reserve study or the reserve contribution in the annual budget
- Adopting rules and regulations of the association, including of pets, parking, and noise
- Preparing monthly financial statements
- Maintaining, repairing, and replacing common area property
- Taking custody of association records
- Deciding to hire an association management company or self-manage the association

Governance of the association includes much more than the above items. However, for the purposes of this chapter, only the duties that relate to analyzing the financial health and quality of life of the association will be covered.

It may help to understand how the association you are considering buying into is governed. If the association is self-managed, all information will be provided to you or your realtor by an officer of the association or, for larger self-managed associations, a person hired to manage on-site. Board members or hired staff are responsible for the duties listed above. A professionally managed association hires an independent management company to assist the board members in performing their duties. In some cases, the board may elect to perform certain duties and hire the management company to perform limited functions.

As mentioned previously, associations are required to hold regular meetings. I have attended hundreds of meetings over the years. I have seen well-run meetings, not so well-run meetings, and disastrous meetings where board members and regular members are screaming at one another and nothing is ever accomplished. Robert's Rules of Order[1] is an effective tool for associations to use. While these rules can be very complex, learning the basic tenets and applying them at association meetings can help things run smoother. (If you would like to become an expert, there are professionals who specialize in Robert's Rules of Order and may consult for a fee.)*

Effective governance should be important to your decision. In many respects, associations are the same as a small city, governed by a local body of officials with wide-ranging powers that can affect you and your quality of life. Picture living in a small town where the mayor and city council are at odds with each other, there is no accountability on spending taxpayer money, and there is uncertainty regarding laws and regulations. (Sounds like your town? Sounds like ones I've lived in too.) Sometimes you have no choice but to live in a dysfunctional town, due to employment or family ties, but buying a condominium can be a decision you make based on all of the facts and circumstances.

How do you know if the association is being governed effectively? If the association board and committees are following best practices, then the association will have less of a chance of running into major issues relating to governance. The end-of-chapter information throughout this book and the information in the appendices will help to inform you about best practices. Those associations that

---

* Please see appendix F for an example of a typical board meeting agenda.

are not following best practices are more likely to run into financial difficulty and are more likely to engage in unhealthy conflicts that may lead to confusion and litigation.

Associations that are governed well should be cooperative in providing requested information and will see your requests as reasonable and part of the normal process when considering a purchase. The Analysis Matrix in chapter 29 lists documents in which you can find each piece of information.

Keep in mind that if you believe the association is not being managed effectively based upon the response and the quality of information provided, please do not think that management will get better after you buy or that you can make a significant difference after you purchase. This may happen, but more likely than not, the culture of the association built up over the years may trump any changes you would like to bring to the association.

Chapter Takeaways

- Board members are volunteers for a job that can be demanding in terms of time and patience.
- Too often associations run out of qualified candidates for the board and end up with available but not as qualified volunteers.
- Decisions of a board should be based on fiduciary responsibility—that is, they should be made based on prudent business decisions.
- A board may be self-managed—that is, without the guidance of professional management; it may use a management company or may hire an on-site manager.
- **Buyers:** Take note of the format of minutes. As detailed in the previous chapter, reading the minutes of the board meetings can be very informative. **Members and Sellers:** The minutes can also alert you to issues to be aware of when anticipating changes

within the association as well as issues that may arise when selling the unit.

Tips—Best Practices

- Governance should be focused on following all provisions of the governing documents; federal, state, and local statutes; as well as the needs of the community. Individual agendas should not dictate policy.
- Board and committee members should consider joining the local chapter of the Community Associations Institute (CAI) and also attend as many training sessions offered by CAI as possible.
- Websites of local chapters of CAI normally list vendors who specialize in providing services to community associations.

Tips—Creating Community

Governance should be transparent, with a method of gaining input from the community.

Further Reading

Managing and Governing: How Community Associations Function, by Clifford J. Treese[2]

11

Legal Issues

Associations are legal entities and normally engage attorneys for a variety of reasons, including collecting delinquent dues, revising governing documents, interpreting provisions of the CC&Rs, and advising the board on potential legal actions and how to respond to legal threats to the association. These activities should not concern a potential buyer of a condominium. However, certain associations have a habit of instigating litigation for a variety of reasons. Some reasons may be valid and beyond the control of the board. Other types of legal action may be at the whim of the board and unnecessary.

Over the past decade, I have seen many associations sue the developer and subcontractors for construction defects and poor materials and workmanship. Early on, these lawsuits were settled out of court with insurance companies not wanting to incur court costs and legal fees. Over the past several years, insurance companies have tended to take associations to court on these lawsuits. As a result, the potential award (after attorney fees) has been diminished. In some cases, associations have been awarded very small amounts, which left the associations with attorney fees in excess of the cash awards.

The fact that an association is involved with a lawsuit is not necessarily a red flag. However, it may be difficult to find out why the association is involved in a lawsuit and what the potential outcome is.

Most types of extraordinary legal action are not discussed in the regular meeting of the board of directors. The board goes into executive session to discuss such matters. Board minutes, if taken, in these sessions may not be discoverable. The only evidence of these meetings would be in the regular board meeting minutes, which may state that the board went into executive session. There may or may not be a short discussion of the executive session once the regular meeting is reconvened. A motion to be voted on by the board in the regular meeting after reconvening may give you an indication of subject areas discussed during executive sessions.

The involvement of attorneys and litigation can be very expensive. Associations generally do not budget adequately for litigation because it is normally not anticipated. This means the cost of litigation, if not paid for by a party other than the association, can reduce funds in the operating budget, may force the association to borrow from reserves, and may require the association to raise dues or to special-assess.

It is not unusual for member faction groups to be formed that oppose certain actions of the board of directors. The actions of faction groups could ultimately be good for the association. However, during the period of unrest, the association could incur a substantial legal fees.

Signs of litigation can be found by reviewing the financial statements and minutes of the association as well as simply by asking if the association is involved in litigation.

Chapter Takeaways

- It is normal for an association to use an attorney for a variety of services. These include interpreting documents and drafting new ones, managing contractual issues, helping with collections, and giving advice concerning issues brought up by owners.
- Some associations seem prone to unnecessary lawsuits, either because of board decisions or because of troublesome owners.
- Boards use executive sessions for discussion of contracts, employee issues, and litigation issues. The sessions are privileged—that is, may not be discoverable.
- The decisions from the executive session are public through a motion in the board minutes, but the reasoning is rarely provided.
- A major source of litigation is due to construction defects. Recoveries often do not include the full amount needed to make repairs, leading to special assessments or increased regular assessments.
- Too often, associations do not plan for legal fees, usually because litigation is not anticipated. Unless the other party ends up paying the attorney fees, the owners have to contribute to cover them.

Tips—Best Practices

- Boards and members should try to reconcile differences without resorting to litigation. Mediation and arbitration, forms of negotiating terms to a dispute, should be considered to help avoid costly litigation.
- **Buyers:** It may be necessary to obtain more information if legal issues come to your attention.

Tips—Creating Community

Litigation should be used only as a last resort. A method of airing disputes and coming to a resolution should be in the policies and procedures manual approved by the board.

Further Reading

- *Conflict Resolution: How ADR Helps Community Associations*, by Mary Avgerinos[1]
- *Changing the Conversation: The 17 Principles of Conflict Resolution*, by Dana Caspersen and Joost Elffers[2]

12

Incorporation

Many states require that associations be incorporated. Incorporation is a legal status that affords associations certain protections in the event of a lawsuit.

Incorporation protects individual members of the association from liability in the event of litigation from a third party. For example, if a member has a party in the association clubhouse and a person attending the party trips on the sidewalk leading to the clubhouse and suffers a debilitating injury, the association may be exposed to a lawsuit for damages.

For the sake of this example, let's say that the insurance policy limit is for $1 million, and the award of damages to the plaintiff is $1.5 million. The association is liable for the difference. Absent the association being incorporated, the plaintiff could collect the $500,000 from each member in total. In this instance, the member with the largest net worth may be the only member who pays the damages.

If the association is incorporated, the association is liable for damages. The association then special-assesses so that each member pays a respective share of the damages based on each member's pro rate share.

Most states have an online register of corporations and each one's current status, and it is very easy to check if the association is incorporated.

Chapter Takeaways

- Incorporating the association provides protection to each member of the association.
- Lack of corporate status may expose individual members to lawsuits; these may come from another member, a vendor, or other individuals.

Tips—Best Practices

- All associations should be incorporated.
- Associations should work with legal counsel and a CPA to ensure that all tax and regulatory filings are kept up-to-date. Most states require an annual update and filing of corporate information along with a fee.

Tips—Creating Community

Adhering to best practices to lessen the liability of the members in the event of a lawsuit serves the asssociation well in establishing a secure and relatively risk-free community.

13

Investment Properties

Buying a condominium for investment purposes may be a good idea under the right circumstances. Keep in mind that renters are required to abide by the same rules as owners. If renters do not follow all rules and regulations, the owner will be fined.

Rental restrictions apply in many condominium associations. These restrictions are very common in vacation areas and can prevent owners from renting out their units a minimum of one week or not being able to rent the unit at all. To be certified to be eligible for FHA lending, associations must abide by restrictions relating to total rentals within the association. Care must be taken to ensure these restrictions do not impede your ability to make a decent rate of return on your investment.

It may be difficult to determine if you will be restricted from renting the investment unit. The CC&Rs may have restrictions such as minimum and maximum lengths of time or absolute restrictions.

Assuming that the documents set an FHA cap, you still need to determine if the association has any rule or regulation concerning rental rotations.

Some associations have a rule that once an owner's tenant terminates the lease, the unit then goes to the bottom of a list of units to be rented. If there is nothing in the bylaws or rules and regulations, it may be due to a number of reasons: the cap has not been reached; when the FHA rule passed, there were already more than the maximum owners renting; or the association has not yet addressed the rule.

FHA lending allows a larger pool of buyers to purchase by providing a smaller down payment and a larger financing pool. Even though there may be no cap when you are considering buying, that does not mean that a cap may not be amended into the association's documents or established via a rule.

Chapter Takeaways

- As a landlord, you have a duty to see that your tenants follow the rules and regulations of the association. If they fail to do so, the association will hold you responsible.
- Governing documents must be read carefully to determine what, if any, restrictions there may be to renting, including minimum stays, maximum time of rentals, and any other restrictions.
- If there is an FHA cap in the documents, be aware of any rules or regulations concerning future buyers when the cap is met.
- Assess the governing documents and any rules and regulations very carefully to make sure you thoroughly understand any process you may need to go through (such as board approval of a tenant).

14

Financial Management

The purpose of this book is not to turn you into an expert on association finances but rather to assist you in looking for red flags that may lead to further questions or may cause a purchaser to look elsewhere. To get us started on finances, I return to familiar territory: best practices. Like most elements of condo ownership, sound financial management of the affairs of the association is aided by adherence to best practices. These financial best practices include but are not limited to:

- Preparing realistic operating budgets
- Considering members not paying dues on time as giving rise to bad debt expense in the budget
- Budgeting for contingencies
- Budgeting for ongoing repairs and maintenance, including inspections of common area components
- Segregating reserve funds from operating funds
- Safeguarding cash and other assets via proper authorizations and check signing

- Proper bidding procedures to help ensure the best price by the most reputable contractors
- Engaging a reserve-study professional
- Following the recommended reserve contributions detailed in the reserve study
- Instituting an effective collection policy to ensure all members pay on time
- Preparing annual federal and state (if applicable) tax returns
- Engaging a certified public accountant to prepare a compiled, reviewed, or audited financial statement

When buying a condominium or a single-family home within an association, a purchaser will become aware of monthly, quarterly, semiannual, or annual dues payable to the association. These dues are called assessments. Assessments are calculated by the board of directors pursuant to budgets. Assessments consist of two budgets: the operating budget and the replacement reserve budget.

Operating Budget

The operating budget takes into consideration day-to-day operational costs such as utilities, insurance, landscaping, management fees, property inspections, and general maintenance. Operating costs are incurred every year.

Replacement Reserve Budget

The replacement reserve budget is derived via the reserve study, more fully explained in chapter 16. The reserve study tells the association how much to put into the reserve bank account each month or year. The purpose of the reserve study is to help ensure that funds are available to pay for future major repairs and replacements, such as the roof and painting.

Sound Financial Management

The theory behind sound financial management is simple: the association needs to assess the members enough money every year to provide adequate funding for all day-to-day operating costs and replacement reserve contributions to ensure the association has enough cash to pay for all expected expenditures. This sounds simple, but in reality it can be very challenging for boards to convince members to pay what is needed. In many cases, the board members themselves are reluctant to increase assessments to properly fund the association due to personal financial obligations.

Associations generally have two bank accounts, the operating bank account and the reserve bank account. The reserve fund may have two bank accounts, capital and noncapital replacement funds, and there may be additional bank accounts under these two categories, such as money market and certificates of deposit. The total operating budget is added to the required contribution to the reserve bank account. This is the total needed to be collected from the members in any given year. Members can pay the same amount for all units, or members may be charged a percentage of the total amount required based on each unit's square footage as compared to the total square footage of the project as documented in the declaration.

Cash shortages on the day-to-day operating accounts become apparent sooner than shortages relating to the replacement reserve. If there are operating fund shortages, associations will not have enough money to pay day-to-day costs. Many times, associations are tempted to borrow money from the replacement reserves to pay day-to-day operating costs. This may help in the short run, but when the roof needs to be replaced, there may not be enough money in the replacement fund. This may lead to a special assessment to pay for the roof. Associations may also, due to day-to-day cash shortages, not perform essential maintenance and inspections on common area property. This deferred maintenance may result in damage to the property and require a special assessment to repair the damage.

Potential buyers should obtain the prior year-end financial statement as well as the most recent financial statement of the association. Year-end financial statements span the period of one year. The most recent interim financial statement would span the period from the last year-end statement to the present.

Financial statements may be prepared by the association treasurer, an outside bookkeeping service, or the association management firm. As a result, the financial statements may not be uniform in appearance from one association to the next. In addition, the financial statement may be prepared on the cash basis, the accrual basis, or the modified cash basis.

Cash Basis

Cash basis financial statements only recognize cash transactions and are handled much the same as an individual's personal checkbook. Revenues are recorded when received and deposited; expenses are recorded when checks are issued. As a result, if members owe money on unpaid dues, this will not be apparent when reviewing cash basis financial statements, nor will amounts owed to vendors.

Accrual Basis

Accrual basis financial statements record revenue when it is earned and expenses when they are incurred. For example, when members are billed for monthly assessments, the association records the amount as income with a corresponding entry to assessments receivable. When members pay the assessment, cash is be recorded with a reduction of the receivable. When a bill from a vendor is received, the expense is recognized with a corresponding increase to accounts payable. When the invoice is paid, the accounts payable account is reduced.

Many people like the accrual method because it more accurately informs you if there are unpaid assessments or unpaid bills. Unpaid assessments may mean the association is in a cash shortfall and may require the members who do pay their assessments to pay more to make up the difference. Unpaid bills may mean the association is not paying bills on time and may be incurring late fees as a result.

Modified Cash Basis

Modified cash basis is a hybrid of the cash method and accrual method.

Balance Sheet

When requesting financial statements, the purchaser should be given at the very least a balance sheet and a revenue and expense statement for the prior twelve-month period ending on the last day of the tax year. The balance sheet lists all assets of the association if the association is on the accrual basis or, if presented on the cash basis, balance in cash in the bank, per the bank reconciliation (much the same as your personal checkbook reconciliation), broken down between operating bank accounts and reserve bank accounts.

Revenue and Expense Statement

The revenue and expense statement spans a particular time period, twelve months if it is a year-end statement and a period between the last year-end statement and the present. Charts 1 and 2, following, show typical balance sheets and statements of revenue expenses for cash basis and accrual basis presentations.

Certainly, accrual basis balance sheets give you more information. However, cash basis financial statements can be supplemented by requesting the assessments receivable subsidiary ledger, which gives you a listing of assessments receivable. You may also want the accounts payable subsidiary ledger containing a listing of unpaid bills. Many associations will provide a statement of revenue and expenses for a period compared to the budget. This report is normally called a variance report, which reports budget-to-actual variances.

Balance Sheet—Cash Basis December 31, 2015

	Operating Fund	Replacement Fund	Total
ASSETS			
Cash, including interest-bearing deposits	$ 9,221	$ 78,605	$ 87,826
Investments	-	40,223	40,223
Total assets	$ 9,221	$ 118,828	$ 128,049
FUND BALANCE	$ 9,221	$ 118,828	$ 128,049

Statement of Revenues and Expenses—Cash Basis
for the Year Ended December 31, 2015

	Operating Fund	Replacement Fund	Total
REVENUES			
Regular assessments	$ 43,124	$ 8,532	$ 51,656
Interest	-	185	185
Late fees	98	-	98
Fines	334	-	334
Total revenues	43,556	8,717	52,273
EXPENSES			
Property maintenance	962	-	962
Utilities	2,180	-	2,180
Landscaping	30,479	-	30,479
Insurance	540	-	540
Management fees	8,568	-	8,568
Professional fees	3,000	-	3,000
Office expense	441	-	441
Bank fees	192	-	192
Licenses and permits	50	-	50
Total expenses	46,412	-	46,412
Excess of revenues over (under) expenses	$ (2,856)	$ 8,717	$ 5,861

Balance Sheet—Accrual Basis December 31, 2015

	Operating Fund	Replacement Fund	Total
ASSETS			
Cash, including interest-bearing deposits	$ 9,221	$ 78,605	$ 87,826
Investments		40,223	40,223
Assessments receivable, net of allowance for doubtful accounts of $25,000	8,600	-	8,600
Prepaid expenses	-	-	-
Total assets	$ 17,821	$ 118,828	$ 136,649
LIABILITIES AND FUND BALANCE			
Accounts payable	$ 1,320	$ 4,580	$ 5,900
Assessments received in advance	4,350	-	4,350
Total liabilities	5,670	4,580	10,250
Fund balance	12,151	114,248	126,399
Total liabilities and fund balance	$ 17,821	$ 118,828	$ 136,649

Statement of Revenues and Expenses—Accrual Basis for the Year Ended December 31, 2015

	Operating Fund	Replacement Fund	Total
REVENUES			
Regular assessments	$ 43,200	$ 8,532	$ 51,732
Interest	-	185	185
Late fees	98	-	98
Fines	500	-	500
Total revenues	$ 43,798	$ 8,717	$ 52,515
EXPENSES			
Property maintenance	962	-	962
Major repairs and replacements	-	4,580	4,580
Utilities	2,180	-	2,180
Landscaping	31,279	-	31,279
Insurance	540	-	540
Management fees	8,568	-	8,568
Professional fees	3,500	-	3,500
Office expense	461	-	461
Bank fees	192	-	192
Licenses and permits	50	-	50
Uncollectible fees	10,000	-	10,000
Total expenses	57,732	4,580	62,312
Excess of revenues over (under) expenses	$ (13,934)	$ 4,137	$ (9,797)

In each method, there are situations that may require additional clarification:

- Low or negative cash balances in the operating or reserve total cash balances may indicate a shortage of cash and require a special assessment.
- If the operating fund owes money to the replacement fund, this may indicate that the operating fund ran out of money and used reserve funds to pay for day-to-day expenses, robbing the reserve fund of needed cash to pay for future repairs and replacements. A special assessment may be needed in the future to fund a major repair or replacement.
- Loans payable to banks may relate to a construction defect issue or underfunding of reserves that required bank financing.
- Expenses greater than revenue in the operating fund, creating a net loss, may indicate the association is not budgeting appropriately, and dues may have to go up as a result. A net loss in the replacement fund revenue and expense statement merely relates to timing of expenditures. As long as the association is following the reserve study–recommended contribution, this is generally not a concern (more fully explained in chapter 16).
- Bad debt expense (accrual basis statements) may be an indication that assessments will need to increase because members are not paying assessments.
- A high balance in assessments receivable (greater than one month of assessments)—an account on accrual basis statements or the total of the assessment receivable subsidiary ledger—may mean assessments will need to increase to subsidize members not paying their dues.
- A large amount of legal fees on the statement of revenue and expenses could mean something as simple as the association restated the governing documents to adhere to state statutes or

may mean the association is involved in a lawsuit. More information is needed to know if there is a potential problem. Reading the minutes may shed light on these types of issues.

- Large amounts of professional fees, including those for engineers and architects, may indicate the association has issues with components. They may also mean the association is headed toward a major issue of repairs and replacements not funded by the reserve bank account. More information is needed.

- Transactions with the developer may mean the association is still under developer control. The association may discover after the developer is gone that the developer has underfunded reserves and dues, which may lead to increased assessments.

- Special assessment income means the association has had to bill the members extra for cash shortfalls, litigation, underfunding reserves, or construction defects.

- Negative fund balance means for each fund, operating and replacement, there are more liabilities than assets.

Please be aware that certain associations are now billing special assessments monthly. The reason for this is that if there is a one-time special assessment and a member is foreclosed on and declares bankruptcy, the association may not be able to collect this assessment. This means that all remaining members will need to make up the difference via increased dues or an additional special assessment. By billing the special assessment monthly, the board ensures that a new member will be liable for all future monthly special assessments.

Tax Returns

Associations are required to file federal, state, and local (if applicable) tax returns. Associations have the option of filing Form 1120H or Form 1120 simply by filing the desired tax return each year.

Associations are obligated to pay tax on income the IRS considers nonexempt/nonmembership income. This is income the IRS believes does not fall within the activities of operating the association for the benefit of the members, such as regular dues, late fees, and special assessments. Potentially, taxable income includes interest income from banks and investments, laundry income, and clubhouse rental.

Associations are allowed to allocate a portion of expenses incurred to help generate nonmember income. Please find income tax matters in the financial concepts of appendix A.

It is often tempting for boards to consider preparing Form 1120H themselves. At first glance, it appears to be a fairly straightforward tax form. However, I strongly suggest a board engage a CPA or licensed tax preparer who specializes in HOA taxation. Recognition of the correct taxable income, allocation of allowable expenses against taxable income, decision to use Form 1120H or Form 1120, and application of applicable IRS code sections and revenue rulings can be crucial in filing an accurate tax return and avoiding paying interest and penalties if audited. The potential savings in the tax preparation fee is negligible when compared to the risk associated with not following all IRS guidelines.

Annual Financial Reporting

General Information

Many associations are subject to annual financial reporting requirements either by governing documents or by state statute. Accountants are engaged to compile, review or audit, and report on the associations' annual financial statements.

Financial Statements

There are three types of assurances CPAs place on financial statements. These assurances, in order of reliance, are:

- **Compilation:** When a CPA compiles financial statements for a client, the CPA presents the information obtained from the client in accordance with generally accepted accounting principles. The CPA does not audit or review the information and places no assurance on the statements. However, if in the course of this preparation the CPA notices anything peculiar about the information, the CPA is required to investigate to satisfy himself or herself that the information would not be misleading to a user.

- **Review:** A review consists of compiling the information into the form of financial statements prepared in accordance with generally accepted accounting principles and applying analytical review procedures to the information to provide limited assurance that nothing came to the attention of the CPA that would lead him or her to believe the statements were not fairly presented. This analysis includes, but is not be limited to, vouching for balance sheet amounts, supporting documentation, and comparing current-year revenue and expense amounts to prior-year and budgeted amounts. This type of assurance is far less than an audit in accordance with generally accepted auditing standards. If the CPA becomes aware of a peculiarity as a result of this review, it is incumbent upon the CPA to perform additional procedures.

- **Audit:** Audited financial statements require the CPA to perform such auditing procedures as promulgated by generally accepted auditing standards to enable the CPA to express an opinion as to the fairness of the financial information. This basically means the CPA will tell you if he or she believes the amounts reported in the financial statements are materially correct. An audit also requires the CPA to document and analyze the system of internal controls inherent in the accounting system. Any weaknesses in internal controls and other operational efficiency comments are normally communicated via a management letter to the board of directors. See chapter 15 for further discussion on financial audits.

Which Form of Reporting Should You Use?

Associations should require at least a yearly compilation. Most large associations require a review or an audit at year-end. Factors in requiring a review or audit are frequently:

1. Requirement in state statutes
2. Requirement in an association's governing documents
3. The time period elapsed from the last audited report
4. Familiarity with the association's management company and ongoing financial information
5. Change in management companies
6. Turnover from the declarant to the board of directors
7. Subsequent change in the board of directors

Preparing for Audit, Review, or Compilation

- Fund balances (retained earnings or members' equity) at the beginning of the year should agree with the fund balances as of the end of the prior year. Any adjustments entered in these accounts should be reconciled.
- Accounts payable should have a positive (credit) balance unless payments were made before the end of the year and bills were entered after the end of the year. The CPA will need this information when performing the audit, review, or compilation.

- The accounts payable aging report balance should agree with the ending general ledger (GL) balance.
- Undeposited cash should only include the balance of cash on hand that has not yet been deposited in the bank by year-end. Payments received on assessments should be applied to owner balances when they are entered into the accounting software, so the balance will not cause undeposited cash to be misstated.
- Accounts receivable should have a positive (debit) balance unless prepaid assessments were entered in the owner's receivable accounts. In that case, separate reports should be generated to show the total of accounts greater than zero (accounts receivable) and the total of accounts less than zero (prepaid assessments). Prior to printing these reports, payments received from owners should be credited to the owners' unpaid balances.
- The accounts receivable aging report balance should agree with the ending GL balance.
- Interest on CDs (certificates of deposit) and other cash accounts should be posted prior to sending the GL and financial statements to the CPA. The board should always be able to get reports on CD balances upon request.
- Financial statements and the GL provided for the financial engagement should be printed directly from the accounting software and should be printed on the same basis of accounting, either accrual basis or cash basis.

Steps in the Compilation, Review, or Audit Process

- An understanding of services to be provided will be established with an engagement letter between the association and its CPA. The association's main point of contact should be indicated. The association's desired due date should be communicated.

- Information will be requested and should be provided to the CPA in a timely manner in order for the audit process to be completed in time to meet the association's desired due date.
- Fieldwork (for audits) date(s) will be scheduled for evaluating the design and implementation of the entity's internal control system and for obtaining adequate information to form an opinion on the financial statements as a whole. This will include interviewing staff, tracing source documents to accounting records, verifying balances, vouching for accounting records to source documents, and comparing accounting records to expectations established during audit planning.
- The CPA will evaluate the audit/review and evidence and may request additional information.
- Finally, the CPA will prepare required reports and communications and issue a financial statement draft. The association's management, including the president and treasurer of the board of directors and the association's managing agent, if applicable, will sign a representation letter stating that the financial statements are the responsibility of management and that management's statements to the auditor during the process are true. If applicable, the CPA may also present proposed adjusted journal entries that are a part of the draft. The proposed adjusted journal entries should be reviewed and approved by management.

Please note that due to independence, CPAs are no longer able to treat the preparation of financial statements as a service included with the audit/review. The CPA may ask the board to designate a competent individual to oversee this "nonattest" service and document this responsibility in the engagement letter.

Signed Documents Required from a CPA

Upon the completion of a financial statement review or audit, the board of director's president and treasurer and the association's managing agent signs a client representation letter and reviews and approves any proposed adjusting journal entries prepared by the CPA.

The client representation letter from the association's management states that all questions and information provided for the review or audit have been answered fully and truthfully and acknowledges that management is responsible for, agrees with, and understands the listed items in the letter.

It is the treasurer's responsibility to ask sufficient questions relating to the information surrounding the proposed adjustments and to perform sufficient due diligence to ascertain the correctness and accuracy of the entries. The treasurer assumes the responsibility of deciding which adjustments to post to the association's books and records. By signing the proposed adjusting journal entries, the treasurer acknowledges that the adjustments are now a part of the association's books and that they should be incorporated in the reviewed or audited financial statements.

A reminder as I wrap up this chapter: associations in sound financial condition follow best practices, assuring cash is always available to meet the financial obligations of the association.

Chapter Takeaways

- Not all associations use financial management best practices.
- Various financial statements and schedules are needed to determine if there are financial concerns.
- Reviewing financial information may lead to the reader asking more questions.

- It is possible that a seller or even the board will not know the association is not following best practices and may be headed for a financial disaster.
- Key account balances and activities can give the reader valuable information.
- **Buyers:** Particular attention should be made to reviewing financial information. A lack of current financial information will impede your ability to make an informed decision regarding purchase.

Tips—Best Practices

- Associations should budget to cover all expenses, including all future replacement and repair expenditures.
- Budgets should include a provision for unexpected expenditures.
- Assessments should be determined based on budgets, not a predetermined amount.
- Members should be allowed access to all financial records.
- Members should engage a qualified certified public accountant or licensed tax preparer to prepare the annual tax filings.
- Members should adhere to all provisions of the CC&Rs and state statutes when engaging a CPA to prepare financial statements.

Tips—Creating Community

Associations should have a method of communicating financial information to the members on an ongoing basis to allow the members to keep abreast of financial matters.

Further Reading

"Treasurer's Handbook," Schwindt & Co.[1]

15

Financial Audits: Necessary Evil or Source of Valuable Information?

Audits provide the highest level of assurance obtainable from a CPA and require the auditor to test the books and records to ascertain the correctness of financial information contained in the statements and notes to the financial statements. One of the major benefits of performing an audit relates to the auditor's requirement to consider the organization's system of internal controls in determining the timing, extent, and nature of tests of transactions. The system of internal controls includes all policies and procedures employed by the board of directors, accounting personnel, and community manager that help protect association assets and help ensure that no one person is in the position of defrauding the association without management detecting the fraud within a reasonable length of time.

No system of internal controls is flawless, and collusion among personnel can make it more difficult to detect fraudulent activities. The CPA is required to communicate weaknesses in the system of internal controls to the board. This is commonly performed in writing via a "communication with those charged with governance" (formerly called the Management Letter). This form of communication is also used to communicate suggestions to improve the financial health of the association, operational efficiencies, and noncompliance with state and federal statutes and regulations.

When analyzing the system of internal controls, auditors commonly look for incompatible duties of accounting personnel and board members. An example of an incompatible set of duties is a bookkeeper who manages all aspects of the accounting process, including billing, depositing, signing checks, preparing bank reconciliations, and preparing financial statements, with little oversight by the manager or board. This person could have the opportunity to take funds from the association and conceal the theft by manipulating the financial records. Strong internal controls include segregating the duties of performing and reviewing financial transactions among association personnel, the community manager, and board members to establish a system of checks and balances to help prevent fraud. Changes in board members, community managers, and accounting personnel require associations to constantly monitor the effectiveness of the system of internal controls. Absent these types of controls, auditors may consider modifying the tests of transactions to compensate for these potential deficiencies.

The true value of an audit is the fulfillment of the fiduciary responsibility of the board in helping to ensure that amounts used in the budgeting and operation phases of the financial process are correct and to ensure the membership that everything possible is being accomplished to protect the financial investment that owners have in their unit and community assets. A board should view an audit as an investment in the financial health of the association, and care should be taken to choose an audit firm with industry experience and the understanding that the evaluation of internal controls and the communication of weaknesses to the board are integral parts of the engagement.

Chapter Takeaways

- A board has a fiduciary duty to the members to ensure the financial health of the association. The involvement of an outside professional, such as a CPA, can help ensure that there are no financial irregularities as well as that there is accuracy of the financial information given to the members.
- Audits, reviews, and compilations prepared by a CPA are not designed to detect fraud. However, if CPAs become aware of fraudulent activities, it is the duty of the CPA to bring such activities to the attention of the board of directors.

Tips—Best Practices

An association that uses an outside CPA to prepare an annual financial statement may lessen the risk of irregularities with respect to financial activities and reporting.

16

Reserve Studies and Funding

O ver the years, I have written numerous articles and have given many seminars on budgeting, reserve funding, and best practices. I am a credentialed reserve study provider, and my firm prepares over two hundred reserve studies annually. The preparation of a reserve study is not an exact science, and there is some disagreement in the reserve study community on how best to fund for future repairs and replacements.

To review, associations prepare two budgets: the operating budget and the reserve budget. The operating budget funds expenditures that occur monthly or yearly. Examples include insurance expenses, utilities, management fees, minor repairs and maintenance, accounting fees, and attorney fees. The reserve budget (detailed in the reserve study) includes expenditures that occur two to thirty years in the future, including replacing the roof; painting the exterior of the buildings; applying the asphalt seal coat and doing major repairs; replacing windows, doors, swimming pool liners, and tennis courts; and conducting major elevator upgrades.

When analyzing the operating budget, you will notice if there is a cash shortfall from year to year. The income statement for the operating budget will show more expenditures than revenue, and the cash balance in the operating bank account will keep getting lower and lower until there is not enough money to pay monthly bills.

Reserve budgets are different. Reserve studies, simply put, consider all expenditures occurring between two and thirty years and determine how much money needs to be saved every year to pay for expenditures, considering inflation and interest income earned on cash balances.

A typical reserve expenditure is replacing the roof on buildings. A roof can last between fifteen and twenty-five years. For many associations, replacing the roof is the most expensive replacement component in the reserve study.

Let's say it would cost $100,000 to replace all roofs if the roofs were replaced today. However, since the roofs will be replaced in twenty years, we need to estimate how much it will cost to replace them in twenty years. Reserve professionals use an inflation factor to estimate the future cost of replacements. Let's assume the calculated future cost of replacing the roofs, including a factor for inflation, is $280,000 (calculation excludes taxes and interest paid/earned on reserve balances). That means the association needs to collect $14,000 ($280,000 divided by twenty years) each year from the members to fund the replacement reserve bank account. If, at the end of twenty years, the association only has $100,000 in the reserve bank account, the association would need to assess $180,000 ($280,000 minus $100,000) to the members to pay for the reserve shortfall. If you use this same calculation on each component, the amount of funding and potential underfunding can become a very large amount.

You can see that the reserve budget shortfall can take years to develop into a problem, whereas the operating shortfall becomes an issue much sooner. Many associations develop a culture of not funding reserves. These reasons include:

- Not wanting to raise dues to fund reserves
- Underbudgeting the operating account and borrowing from reserves
- Not preparing a reserve study that tells the board how much to save
- Not including all major expenditures in the reserve study
- Not updating the reserve study annually to adjust for changes in costs and inflation
- Creating a culture of special assessing the members for major expenditures
- Not establishing a cash cushion (contingency) in the reserve bank account to shield the association from unexpected expenditures (dry rot, damage due to storms, etc.)
- Not adequately maintaining and inspecting common area property so components last as long as they should (more fully explained in chapter 17)

So, how do you determine if an association is underfunded and heading toward a special assessment?

The best way to determine if an association is underfunded is to review the reserve study. If the reserve study is prepared by a credentialed provider (an RS, Reserve Specialist, or PRA, Professional Reserve Analyst), you can determine the study was prepared using guidelines promulgated by both sponsoring organizations. This means the study is more likely to contain all applicable components to be replaced, that the replacement costs estimates are from reasonable sources, and the cash flow model provides for funding at least to pay for all repairs and major replacements over a given period, generally thirty years. If the reserve study is prepared by an uncredentialed person or firm, including a board member or committee of the association, it is less likely to be correct.

Reserve studies prepared by credentialed providers are prepared using three different levels of assurance:

- A level I reserve study, the highest level of assurance, requires a site visit, which includes inventorying all components, taking measurements of components, considering the condition of components, listing the components using current replacement costs and estimated useful lives, and building a cash flow model that includes inflation and interest earned from reserve balances.
- A level II reserve study is an onsite update and is much the same as a level I; however, the reserve study provider does not measure the components. A level II updates the study with respect to components, replacement costs, estimated useful lives, timing of replacements, inflation, and interest earned. Please note that a site visit is a cursory review of the condition of association components. It is not a complete building envelope inspection (discussed under maintenance in chapter 17). A person on a site visit is concerned with seeing if components appear to be wearing as intended. A site visit does not include the consideration of design, materials, or workmanship.
- A level III reserve study is an off-site update that reviews the same areas as a level II study; however, the reserve study provider does not visit the property to consider the condition of the components.

All three levels of assurances have one very important thing in common: they compute needed assessment from the members to ensure that there are sufficient funds available to pay for expenditures in the year the work is completed and to repair or replace common area components such as painting, roof replacement, asphalt, and decks.

Reserve studies can be voluminous and contain many schedules and graphs. If you can get a copy of the reserve study, please look for the cash flow model.

The following is an example of a reserve study cash flow model:

Cash Flow Method—Threshold
Funding Model Projection $50,000

Beginning Balance: $263,155

Year	Annual Contribution	Annual Interest	Annual Expenditures	Projected Ending Reserves	Fully-Funded Reserves	Percent Funded
2010	70,350	4,623	72,119	266,008	465,172	57%
2011	71,933	6,153		344,094	502,978	68%
2012	73,551	5,176	127,363	295,459	472,948	62%
2013	75,206	6,783		377,449	572,246	65%
2014	76,898	8,365	4,546	458,166	669,014	68%
2015	78,629	5,543	226,007	316,331	546,933	57%
2016	80,398	7,261		403,990	652,955	61%
2017	82,207	9,050		495,247	761,118	65%
2018	84,056	9,512	69,378	519,438	802,264	64%
2019	85,948	8,417	148,829	464,975	766,558	60%
2020	87,881	9,060	63,592	498,324	818,536	60%
2021	89,859	11,038		599,220	936,438	63%
2022	91,881	10,692	119,098	582,696	937,918	62%
2023	93,948	12,475	15,384	673,734	1,045,586	64%
2024	96,062	14,646		784,442	1,171,122	66%
2025	98,223	12,370	224,611	670,424	1,075,172	62%
2026	100,433	10,997	179,849	602,005	1,032,021	58%
2027	102,693	13,270		717,968	1,159,215	61%
2028	105,004	12,625	149,175	686,422	1,146,393	59%
2029	107,366	12,216	139,170	666,834	1,146,672	58%
2030	109,782	10,543	203,775	583,384	1,085,757	53%
2031	112,252	12,999		708,634	1,231,500	57%

(Continued)

Beginning Balance: $263,155 (*Continued*)

Year	Annual Contribution	Annual Interest	Annual Expenditures	Projected Ending Reserves	Fully Funded Reserves	Percent Funded
2032	114,778	14,614	46,589	791,437	1,333,734	59%
2033	117,360	9,457	386,265	531,989	1,100,347	48%
2034	120,001	12,046		664,036	1,256,311	52%
2035	122,701	2,825	590,354	199,207	826,784	24%
2036	125,461	2,106	162,626	164,148	828,635	19%
2037	128,284	4,712		297,144	996,431	29%
2038	131,171		377,795	50,520	791,968	6%
2039	134,122	2,482		187,123	968,799	19%

The model starts with the cash in the reserve fund at the beginning of the year; the suggested contribution to reserves (the amount the association should contribute to reserves for the current or next budget year); the expected expenditures from the account for each year; the interest earned; and the expected ending balance for the current or budget year and each subsequent year. The projected ending balance of reserves for each year may accumulate until it is time to pay for a major project. Reserve funding plans should provide for all expenditures, never allowing the ending balance to go below zero. Most associations allow for fluctuations in prices and other surprises by never allowing the ending balance to drop below a specific amount.

The first thing to look for in the cash flow model is that the ending balance never drops below zero. The next thing to notice is the required contribution for each year. Is it the same each year, or does the required contribution increase each year? If the required contribution increases each year, you should expect your dues to increase proportionately for the reserve contribution portion of your dues. This is not necessarily a bad thing. You would expect dues to increase a little each year to keep up with inflation. However, if you see a large lump sum contribution in any year in the future, expect to pay this with a special assessment.

Also, read the narrative for each major component, including roofs, siding, windows, doors, decks, and asphalt. Look for recommendations for a complete building envelope inspection. This may indicate the reserve study provider is not sure about suspected structural issues and is suggesting the association get a second opinion from an architect or engineer. This should be a major concern.

Chapter Takeaways

- A reserve study is a savings plan for future repairs, major maintenance, and replacement of common area items.
- Reserve studies should be prepared by an analyst with the designation of RS (Reserve Specialist) or PRA (Professional Reserve Analyst).
- Properly funded reserves help avoid a major financial crisis for both the association and the individual owners.
- The cash flow page of the reserve study should never show a negative balance.
- Other concerns are chronic underfunding of reserves, not updating the study each year, and revising the analyst's estimates of time to repair or cost to repair.
- **Buyers:** The lack of sufficient reserves is one of the main reasons for the necessity of a special assessment. Particular attention should be paid to reserves and information in this chapter.

Tips—Best Practices

- Associations should prepare a reserve study and update the study annually.
- The association should fund the replacement reserve bank account according to the recommended contribution specified in the reserve study.

- The association should not borrow from the reserve bank account to pay for operating expenses.
- The association should only engage qualified experts to perform the reserve study.
- The association should engage an engineer or architect to perform a complete building envelope inspection.

Tips—Creating Community

The association should always fund the reserve bank account according to the reserve study. This helps avoid a special assessment, which can create drama and distrust among members.

Further Reading

- *Best Practices Report #1: Reserve Studies/Management*, published by the Foundation for Community Association Research[1]
- *Reserve Funds: How & Why Community Associations Invest Assets*, by Mitchell H. Frumkin, PE, CGP, and Nico F. March, CFM, RRP[2]

17

Property Maintenance and Condition Assessment

Associations are charged with the responsibility of maintaining common area property. This type of ongoing maintenance can include keeping the roof free of debris and mold, caulking windows and doors, maintaining gutters and downspouts, and regularly inspecting association property.

Certain states require the preparation of a maintenance plan. Many associations rely on the professional community management company to perform needed maintenance procedures. Some associations, due to monetary constraints or just not paying attention, perform very little ongoing maintenance.

Some places may look nice because of landscaping and fresh paint. However, this may be deceiving. The association may not be paying attention to ongoing maintenance procedures that can help extend the useful life of a component or inspections that can bring to light issues that need attention before they become much more expensive to repair.

Some associations retain the services of an engineering or architecture firm to perform a complete building envelope inspection on association property. This inspection considers original materials, design and workmanship, as well as the current condition of the property, which can aid the reserve study provider in knowing the useful lives of components.

The complete building envelope inspection can be a useful tool in determining if the association is currently or will eventually have problems with association property. However, most associations do not have this report. Reserve studies, previously discussed, give a general indication of the condition of association property; however, this is most often far less than the much more extensive condition assessment report.

Very often, the association does not know the current condition of association components, which may have an impact on a future special assessment. A buyer should obtain more information about the condominium than just the unit to be purchased.

This can be accomplished very simply. When you engage a home inspector to look at the unit being purchased, suggest the inspector increase his fee to walk the property to gain an understanding of the overall condition of the association property: the exterior of buildings, decks, asphalt, retaining walls, and all other property, including swimming pools, clubhouse, tennis courts, et cetera. Do not require comments on this be in the report. Merely walk the grounds with this person and take notes.

Questions to ask include:

- What is the overall condition of association property, including all buildings, asphalt, clubhouse, swimming pool, tennis courts, landscaping, retaining walls, drainage, and what any other comments the inspector would like to offer on those?
- Does it look like the association is adequately maintaining the property?

- When will the roof, gutters, paint, asphalt, windows, siding, and doors need to be replaced or repaired?
- Would you buy into this community?

Chapter Takeaways

- Associations are responsible for the day-to-day maintenance of the common property.
- Many associations do not have a maintenance plan even though the importance of regular maintenance cannot be overstated.
- A complete building envelope inspection may highlight areas of concern.
- A building inspector may help with information on the condition of common area property.
- **Buyers:** It is difficult to determine the condition of common area property without engaging an architect or engineer to perform a complete building envelope inspection. It may be worth the money to engage a property inspector to walk the property with you.

Tips—Best Practices

- The association should create a maintenance plan and follow the procedures.
- The association should engage an architect or engineer to perform a complete building envelope inspection.

Tips—Creating Community

The association should strive to maintain the property and grounds at the highest level to foster pride in the community.

18

New Construction and Conversion Issues

New condominiums are constructed by a developer and a team of subcontractors. Developers find the land, design and build the condominiums, and are in control of the association until turnover, typically when 75 percent of all of the condominiums in the project are sold.

The association does not change during turnover. The only thing that changes during turnover is the control of the board of directors. Prior to turnover, the developer and his or her team have the majority votes on the board and make all of the decisions of the association. These decisions include determining budgets, how much to contribute to reserves, and maintenance procedures and addressing architectural review issues. Once turnover takes place, the members assume control of the association by occupying the majority of the seats on the board of directors.

During developer control, it may be difficult to obtain necessary information. Budgets, financial statements, and reserve studies are sometimes prepared by the developer, and because projects are new, support for budget line items may be missing.

Newly Constructed Condominiums

Newly constructed condominiums present a different set of issues to a prospective buyer.

The good news is that the association is starting from year one to save for future repairs and replacements. Therefore, there is less chance that reserves will be underfunded. Also, developers will do everything they can to make the condominium attractive to potential buyers by keeping assessments low and offering incentives for purchasers.

The bad news about newly constructive condominiums is this:

- The developer may keep assessments artificially low to help spur sales. This may mean that the developer is subsidizing operating assessments, and once the developer is gone, assessments may increase dramatically. The developer accomplishes this by making up the difference between assessments to members and actual costs incurred to run the association. Once the developer is gone, a new reserve study may indicate reserves are too low, requiring an increase in assessments.

- The developer may rely on subcontractors to construct the condominium. The developer may not hire an independent consultant, due to cost constraints, to oversee the subcontractors and ensure best practices and adequate workmanship.

- Construction defect issues may not become apparent for years, long after the developer is gone.

- If construction issues are discovered before turnover, developers may opt to perform limited solutions rather than address more costly permanent fixes to association property.

- The developer may not keep finances separated from the developer's business and the association. This may lead to the developer owing the association money due to borrowing funds, not paying the developer's share of assessments during the time of developer control, or using association personnel to work on developer duties, including sales and punch lists to new buyers. (Punch lists are work performed by the developer, generally on the inside of the units, such as fixing squeaky floors and cosmetic issues. Punch lists are not the responsibility of the association.)
- The developer may not use best practices with respect to finances and managing the association. Many developers choose to use the services of a community management company to help manage the association. This may give a purchaser an added layer of protection from potential issues.

Conversion Condominiums

Conversion condominiums are apartments subsequently converted to condominiums. The age of the apartments at the time of conversion varies. The good news about conversion condominiums is that they are attractively priced and are in close-in or unique areas that do not have land available to build new condominiums. Some are historic structures in wonderful urban areas that afford the purchaser a unique lifestyle. The bad news is they used to be apartments and may have issues that are not resolved by the developer during the conversion process.

It should be noted that many developers use the highest level of best practices and are very conscientious in constructing new condominiums or converting existing apartments. The problem is that you may not know if you are dealing with one of these wonderful developers. Realtors, community managers, and other professionals in the industry may provide insight to top-notch developers in your area. Buyers can also search keywords, such as the names of the association, developer, lawsuit, et cetera, to see if there are any issues with the association or the developer. It may be difficult to ascertain the developer of older associations, but it is worth investigating.

Chapter Takeaways

- New construction and conversion properties present additional concerns and pitfalls.
- Developers may subsidize assessments, which may mean a big increase at turnover.
- Conversion properties may have deferred maintenance issues that could result in a future special assessment.

Tips—Best Practices

Shortly after turnover, the board should have a complete building inspection by an engineer or architect.

Further Reading

- *Construction Defect Litigation: The Community Association's Guide to the Legal Process*, by Ross W. Feinberg, Esq., and Ronald L. Perl, Esq.[1]
- *Home and Condo Defects: A Consumer Guide to Faulty Construction*, second edition, by Thomas E. Miller, Rachel M. Miller, and Mathew T. Miller[2]

19

Insurance

Buyers of condominiums should be aware that insurance for the condominium is different from insurance for a single-family home. Depending on the legal framework of the condominium or townhouse and the CC&Rs, insurance needs may differ. Generally, the owner of the condominium insures within the four walls of his or her condominium, and the association insures everything from the middle of the wall studs outward, including the roof, siding, and grounds. Insurance questions asked by owners of condominiums should be about deductible and coverage limits, cash or replacement value, contents, and flood and wind damage coverage.

Each condominium and homeowners association requires a master policy, which may include but not be limited to information on general liability, property, directors and officers liability, demolition and increased cost of construction, backup of sewer and drain, crime and fidelity, computer fraud insurance, workers compensation, earthquake coverage, commercial umbrella coverage, as well as other coverages recommended to the board by an experienced agent.

This discussion is meant to allow you to begin familiarizing yourself with coverages available for the buyer and the association. I'm not an insurance professional and in no way present this information as an all-inclusive discussion of insurance and coverage.

Chapter Takeaways

Insurance needs of associations are complicated and need the involvement of experts.

Tips—Best Practices

- Hire a highly respected insurance agent or broker who specializes in providing insurance to condominium and homeowners associations.
- Meet with the agent at least annually to discuss the history and current activities of the association.
- When meeting with the agent, discuss all existing policies and all potential polices the association should consider. Work with the agent to consider the cost and benefit of each additional policy and determine which policies are appropriate.
- Create an insurance binder with all policies and an executive summary of all coverages.
- Document the meeting with the agent, the decisions reached, and the business rationale of existing coverages.
- Communicate coverage to members so that they may use this information in determining their insurance needs.

20

Online Banking, Cyber Theft, and Internal Controls

O ver the past several years, I have become increasingly aware of the potential of theft occurring when associations are involved with online banking. One of the greatest areas of concern is fraudulent electronic funds transfers (EFT) and ACH transaction fraud. Cyber criminals are now targeting associations due to the ease of accessibility because of weak or nonexistent controls.

Many associations are implementing online activities without considering the necessity of additional internal controls. If the fraud can be traced to a security breach in the victim's computer (for example, viruses, malware [malicious software programs], or hijacking programs), the bank may be able to avoid responsibility for the recovery of the lost funds. The bank also may find that the customer is not in compliance with its security authentication procedures, which also may impair the victim's ability to recover lost funds.

External Attacks

Computer systems without effective firewalls and software protections to prevent criminals from accessing systems are at risk. In the past, cyber criminals primarily gained access through malware imbedded within email attachments. This was relatively simple to counter by simply not opening attachments from untrusted sources (though this assumes the sender also has good IT practices). These days, malware is more commonly found in website banner ads. Often these make their way onto reputable sites. For example, Facebook, NYTimes.com, and Yahoo! have all been victims of such poisoned ads. As such, you should never assume a site or email is safe. You should always install any software updates available (even if it sometimes means the inconvenience of restarting the computer). Even an up-to-date machine can be vulnerable if the user is tricked into providing confidential information to a malicious website. Phishing emails posing as legitimate messages from the bank or a website the association does business with will try to get the victim to enter the username and password or other sensitive information on a site that may look exactly like a legitimate site. As a general rule, no bank, email provider, government agency, or any other major institution will ever request personal information via email.

Limiting Access

All systems, especially the computer used to conduct online banking, should be protected by a firewall and monitored with updated security software. Access to online banking computers should be limited and incorporate all the proper physical and logical access controls including policies and procedures. In smaller association settings, using a computer that is not set up on a routing system to allow for wireless access may not be practical. Routers that require a security name are at risk by sophisticated hackers. Changing the association's router's administrative and Wi-Fi passwords from the default settings to something more secure can help prevent such attacks. If the equipment was issued by the association's internet service provider, technical support should be able to help change this feature. If the association purchased its router from another vendor, it may be necessary to contact the manufacturer if there are questions about making these changes. Physical controls to the computer and proper passwords (including numbers, letters, and special characters) that are changed periodically are necessary.

Internal Attacks

An effective system of internal controls includes the segregation of responsibilities involving financial transactions. This is especially true when it comes to online banking activities. Auditors refer to duties that are not segregated as incompatible duties. An example of an incompatible set of duties would be a bookkeeper who manages all aspects of the accounting process including billing, making deposits, signing checks, preparing bank reconciliations, and preparing financial statements with little oversight by the manager or board. This person could have the opportunity to take funds from the association and conceal the theft by manipulating the financial records.

Strong internal controls include segregating the duties of performing and reviewing financial transactions among association personnel, community manager, and board members to establish a system of checks and balances to help prevent fraud. Changes in board members, community managers, and accounting personnel require associations to constantly monitor the effectiveness of the system of internal controls. Many associations have strong controls as they pertain to traditional activities such as paying bills by check. These same controls should be incorporated into the system when online activities are activated.

One of the controls many banks use to deter cyber theft is to authenticate the online transaction by a phone call or email to the person designated to authorize the transaction. However, if the person designated to authorize the transaction is also the person who has the ability to perpetrate and conceal the transaction, such as the bookkeeper, this valuable control is diminished. It is sometimes not practical to have a person designated for an online transaction who is not a member of the financial team. However, the person authorizing the transaction should not be able to make entries or adjustments to the books and records. If possible, the person authorizing the transaction should be contacted by email on a separate computer with different login credentials.

Regardless of the segregation of duties, monitoring and reconciling EFT/ACH accounts daily is important to quickly identify unauthorized transactions and to enable the association to reverse fraudulent transactions.

The following steps may be effective in developing controls:

- Perform a risk assessment including external and internal cyber theft fraud attributes.
- Dedicate a computer or system for online banking.
- Log and monitor key computers or systems.
- Segregate online banking functions.
- Reconcile EFT/ACH transactions daily.
- Consider a clearing bank account and make transfers from a separate system.
- Work with the bank to develop and understand security authentication procedures.
- Work with the independent auditor to understand effective internal control procedures.

Many banks are now scrambling to increase controls over layered security, anomaly detection, administrative controls, and customer awareness. Homeowners associations should also be diligent in assessing and addressing cyber theft issues and related controls.

Responding to EFT fraud may require both technical and operating expertise. Trojan horse programs designed to facilitate these crimes are often difficult to detect and remove. In addition, an in-depth understanding of transaction and data flow throughout the EFT process plays a critical role in discovery.

Chapter Takeaways

- Cyber theft continues to be a threat for associations.
- Associations should consider hiring an independent consultant to perform a cyber-risk assessment.
- Outside professionals, such as IT consultants, CPAs, and bankers, may assist in developing adequate internal controls (further reading: www.cybersafekeeping.com).

21

FHA Certification

The Federal Housing Administration (FHA) under the auspices of HUD requires associations to apply for certification in order for buyers of condominiums within the association to use FHA-insured loans. In other words, if you want to sell your unit and the association has successfully qualified for FHA certification, the potential purchaser will be able to borrow using an FHA loan. FHA loans are beneficial to sellers. They allow for a greater number of potential buyers due to relaxed income qualification ratios and the allowance of blemishes on credit reports.

In order to qualify for FHA certification, associations must meet certain criteria, including minimum amounts contributed to reserves, minimum number of members who are delinquent on paying dues, and maximum number of rental properties.

Because the threshold for meeting most of the criteria for certification is fairly low, it is a concern if the association is not certified. Associations may fail to be certified because of the minimum number of delinquencies. Another common reason for certification failure is the threshold of rental properties to owner-occupied properties. If you are an investor, this may not be a concern. If you are a homeowner, this could be a major concern on resale.

Buyers of condominiums should ask if the association has been certified by HUD to allow FHA loans. If the association is not certified, the buyer should ask why the association has failed the requirements if the association has applied.

Chapter Takeaways

* FHA certification may be a positive indication of financial health.
* If an association is not HUD approved, future buyers may be forced to seek conventional loan products, which may affect salability.
* **Buyers:** If you are planning on buying a condo, you should ask if the association has been certified by HUD to allow FHA loans. If the association is not certified and has applied, you should ask why the association has failed the requirements.

22

Timeshares

Timeshare was a term coined in the United Kingdom in the early 1960s for shared ownership of vacation property. Originally used by groups of families buying a property, the idea soon caught on with developers who saw the potential of building destination resorts and selling a resort room for one-fiftieth ownership with two weeks off for repairs and upgrades, along with a maintenance fee to each owner.

The first timeshares in the United States was started in 1974 by Caribbean International Corporation, offering what it called a twenty-five-year "vacation license" in resorts that it owned in Florida, St. Croix, and St. Thomas. The contract was fairly clean and simple. The owner had a twenty-five-year period of time in a specific season and for a specific number of weeks, plus a $15 per diem fee and a $25 switching fee to use one of the other resorts. In any given year, the owner could use the time, rent it to someone else, or gift it for any year, but the property used or not, the per diem fee was owed.

Florida stepped in shortly thereafter, requiring, among other things, that these timeshares were to be fee-simple ownership with a maintenance fee. Currently, all countries that have such resorts have some type of regulation in place. Some countries are restrictive in matters of foreign ownership of property, and over time, the result has been two paths of ownership. The one path that has remained fairly constant has been deeded ownership. The second is right to use contracts.

With deeded ownership, the owner may do whatever that owner desires: use the week, rent it out to another, give it away, leave it to heirs, or sell to another buyer. The owner is also liable for a share of real estate taxes and maintenance fees. Given that resorts may be in foreign countries, issues of property law may make understanding ownership complex. It may include such variations as leasehold ownership for a period of time, after which ownership reverts to the seller—either the developer or another corporation that purchased from the developer.

Right to use contracts are for a specified period of time. After the period ends, all rights reside with the owner. Often the contract is represented as a club membership or the right to use the reservation system. Care needs to be taken with the latter. If the company operating the reservation system is not the company that owns the property, and the reservation company ceases to exist, all rights may be lost.

There are variations on both types of timeshares. Disney Vacation Club is one example of a variation on the right to use contract. The buyer receives an undivided interest in the property plus an annual allotment of vacation points, which may be used to stay at other Disney resorts, saved for a future year, or even borrowed from future years.

Depending on the company's approach, the time may be fixed for the same period every year, float within a series of weeks (and subject to availability), or rotate, which gives a different specific week each year.

Points programs are sold based on the assigned value of a piece of property. If a company owns multiple locations, it will rate each location on a point system. Buying points relative to one of the more popular locations normally costs more, which then provides more points, thus providing a longer stay at a lower point destination. The reverse is also true; buying based on a lower cost, destination, or season may result in one not having enough points to stay at the more popular destination. Borrowing points from the future may ameliorate the matter.

There are a number of criticisms leveled at the timeshare concept. Many say they are overpriced. It is estimated that 50 percent or more of the cost of a timeshare purchase goes to marketing, sales, and other fees. Realistically, this can never be recovered by a purchaser. Another complaint is that the maintenance fees (which include property taxes) are too high.

Often, the comparison is between staying in a hotel and owning a timeshare. What is not considered is the mortgage payment, maintenance fees, and any preset vacation schedule.

Perhaps the most severe criticism, however, is the impression many get of the sales staff, similar to a used-car sales force, and the high-pressure "buy today as this offer won't last!" sales technique.

While timeshares can be sold, most do not appreciate in value. With the high cost of marketing and sales commissions, and difficulty in marketing the remaining contract or deed oneself, often at a nominal price as low as one dollar, it is difficult to exit from the contract or deed. Simply walking away and stopping payment on maintenance fees may cause you to be pursued for collection of these fees. And while there are third-party groups that will offer to sell, they typically want upfront costs, which are nonrefundable and not dependent on the final price achieved, if any. In spite of all of this, however, timeshares—deeded or right of use—are indeed popular with many people.

Chapter Takeaways

- Timeshares are unlike most property investments, as they most likely will only lose value over time.
- Timeshares may be deeded property or right of use, and hybrids of the two exist.
- Sales tactics are often high pressure for a decision that could affect many years to come.

Tips—Best Practices

- Do extensive research before attending a session with a sales group and be prepared for high-pressure tactics. Find out the cost of the prospective program, prices of similar timeshares, and sale prices on the timeshares you have selected.
- Consider buying from another purchaser, but perform due diligence: investigate the property, talk with the prior owner, and contact the developer or management company of the property.
- Before you purchase a resale, determine that there is no attached debt from the prior owner.
- On a resale, contact the management company and determine if all rights transfer, such as use of name hotels and loyalty points.

Further Reading

- *RCI Points User Guide: Tips, Tricks and Secrets: A Practical Guide to Understanding and Using RCI Points*, by Allen Kelley[1]
- *Timeshare Tips & Tricks: Stay at 5 Star Resorts for Pennies, Eliminate Maintenance Costs, Trade, and What to Do When You Don't Want It Anymore*, by Vincent Lehr[2]

23

Cooperatives

A housing cooperative, or co-op, offers a distinct form of home ownership with many characteristics differing from the usual forms of ownership—single-family, condominiums, and rentals.

Property in a co-op is owned by a corporation, and the members (owners) are granted shares in the organization. One primary advantage of co-ops is that the buying power is compounded, thus lowering the cost per member for repairs, maintenance, and related items.

A rather unique aspect of co-ops is that future occupants are screened and accepted (or not accepted) to live there.

There are two general ways in which one may live in a co-op: nonownership (called nonequity or continuing) and ownership (called equity or strata). Nonownership occupancy is by a lease or occupancy agreement. Ownership occupancy may be through a purchase agreement and legal documents registered on the general title.

A cooperative may also refer to what is found across the United States in some colleges and universities, where a building is owned by a cooperative organization, and students rent bedrooms and have access to communal resources.

Many housing cooperatives model on a cooperative attitude and approach among its members, with volunteers to take care of as much as possible in ongoing maintenance and repairs. However, as a legal entity, the co-op may contract with outside vendors to accomplish necessary work, including maintenance and management.

Because in nonequity and limited-equity cooperatives members do not own real estate, but rather shares in the corporation, states have drafted legislation specific to how they are operated and the rights and liabilities of shareholders.

In nonequity co-ops, the right to a specific unit is by way of occupancy agreement or proprietary lease. In an equity co-op, ownership is by title transfer. The co-op, since it holds title to the entire property, has the responsibility for maintenance; as it is a nonprofit, work is done at cost.

Decisions are made by a board of directors. In some circumstances, shareholders are limited to one vote per shareholder; in others, shareholders may hold more than one share. Politics may vary from one co-op to another, but generally a majority vote of the board decides issues. In small co-ops, all members may be on the board; in larger ones, the size of the board is limited.

As a housing co-op is normally nonprofit, income is approximately equal to costs. As long-term repairs will need to be made, just as in condominiums and PUDs, there should be reserves for future expenditures. And because the co-op is normally a corporation, it is possible that it could have other sources of income; these should reduce lease and other costs to occupants.

Starting a co-op may be difficult when it is not organized by a developer. The sizeable mortgage needs someone to back it to the satisfaction of the bank. Additionally, it may take a year or more to create organizational policies, particularly if this is a random group of people with no previous experience. Often the group is already having pressure on whatever existing housing they have. They may be organized by a group of tenants when the building owner wishes to sell.

Resale value of a unit may be market rate or limited equity. With market rate, the owner may sell at whatever price the market will bear. Financing may be similar to a condominium unit, with the exception that the co-op may carry the mortgage. Usually the difference in price between a co-op market rate and a condominium is that the co-op typically is much lower.

With a limited-equity unit, the co-op has rules as to the price of shares when sold. The idea behind a limited-equity co-op is to provide and maintain affordable, low-cost housing. With no-equity housing, there is a very low purchase price, with a monthly fee in lieu of rent; when sold, all that is returned is that very low fee (similar to a security deposit).

Both condominiums and co-op housing have rules and regulations imposed by governing documents and enforced by a board of directors. One of the differences is that in a condominium, an individual owns the interior and is able to remodel as long as it does not impact structural issues. In a co-op, one does not own the interior but rather has the right to use; remodeling likely requires permission of the board. Permission may be withheld for structural reasons or simply political ones.

Because of the group ownership of the entire project, and the fact that, at its base, a co-op requires collaboration and teamwork, the board or a committee has the power to screen new owners. This can make selling an interest in the co-op difficult.

Despite the potential difficulties, co-ops remain a solid investment in large urban areas such as New York and often result in solid appreciation. If the board and members adhere to best practices, a co-op can be a wonderful investment and living experience.

Chapter Takeaways

- Ownership in a co-op may be by equity or nonequity.
- With a market rate co-op, the value of the price may increase or decrease as the general market does; with a limited-equity co-op, share prices may be controlled by the co-op to maintain low-cost housing.
- Unlike condos, for which each owner obtains his or her own financing, in a co-op there is one mortgage on the entire property.
- Similar to condos, there is an operating budget and reserves for repairs, which owners pay through fees.
- Co-ops have control through the approval process over who may purchase.

Tips—Best Practices

Purchasers need a clear understanding of the requirements for collaboration and teamwork involved in a co-op and of the community personality and temperament. One is not just buying into a building but also into a community with which one is expected to associate on a day-in, day-out basis.

Tips—Creating Community

Boards and members practicing transparency in governance and activities can go a long way toward creating a vibrant, supportive, and engaging community.

24

Manufactured Home Communities

Manufactured home communities all too often bring up an immediate image of "trailer trash"—single-wide units with rusty exteriors and plastic flowers on the porch. That image, particularly in areas of very high home costs, is changing significantly.

In the Malibu area of California, with single-family homes running in the $20 million to $40 million range, homes in the Paradise Cove Mobile Home Park were reported in the $1.25 million to $3.75 million range, according to the *Wall Street Journal* in August of 2014.[1] Of course, it didn't hurt that the homes sat on a bluff overlooking the Pacific Ocean.

Approximately 10 percent of housing in the United States is in manufactured or manufactured homes. While manufactured homes have a history of declining value as opposed to other forms of homes, this may be changing due to better manufacturing processes, designs that don't shout "manufactured home," and more and better interiors and upgrades.

In a manufactured home park, the land is leased, normally from a corporation, and the manufactured home sits on a temporary foundation while retaining the axels underneath. Some states have enacted laws to protect lessees should the lessor decide to terminate the land lease. Oregon, for example, has enacted a series of statutes setting out the process if a lessor decides to convert the land to a planned community subdivision of manufactured dwellings, and another series of statutes should the land be converted to other uses.

As landlord, the lessor may have certain responsibilities according to state statutes and there may be certain prohibitions to acts by the landlord, or specific processes that person must go through when there is a lessor/lessee conflict. Overall, the laws are similar to those regulating apartment rentals.

The lease sets out the rights and responsibilities of the parties.

Conversion of a manufactured home park to a planned community subdivision of manufactured homes will include CC&Rs to be recorded over the entire plat and, depending on state law, may result in an entity similar to a PUD or to a condominium or, if the parties are creative, possibly a co-op. Conversion is definitely not a given but is usually driven by increasing values of the land due to urban and suburban growth.

Chapter Takeaways

- The expansion of prebuilt or prefab homes has expanded the market for manufactured homes, with many comparable to single-family homes.
- In some circumstances, rising land values and growth of communities is pressuring some manufactured home parks to be bought out by developers and closed.
- Developers looking to start more upscale communities, including retirement communities, are creating upscale manufactured home parks.

25

Master Community Associations

Master associations are created when two or more developers join together over a large plot of land and subdivide it into separate parcels to be developed as separate subassociations. The master association may or may not include any homes within it.

For example, a master association could include a plat of land with an entrance gate, roads within it, a mix of single-family and townhome-style homes, and within the overall boundaries, a separate plat of land that was platted and developed as a condominium community. The master budget would include the roads and gates and any community resources, such as a community building and other recreational facilities. All owners within the master association, including the condominium, would pay a pro rata share of the maintenance of those items. The master, in turn, would have a subbudget for the townhomes' maintenance.

In this circumstance, there are two boards of directors, one for the condominium and one for the master; in many, if not most, circumstances, there might be one or more positions on the board of the master association specifically reserved for the condo owners. Owners of the condominiums pay dues to their own association for maintenance and repairs and dues for common areas of the master association, which they share with everyone else.

Another example of a master association is one in which there are several subassociations, with the master association only responsible for maintenance and repairs to common areas used by all of the subassociations. In this case, all subassociations pay their own dues, plus a proportional amount to the master for its dues.

Master communities may also include high-rise condominiums consisting of commercial properties on the first level with residential condominiums on the upper levels. Both groups have unique budgeting and reserve contribution needs. Typically, a master association is created with two members, the commercial group and the residential group. The master association funds expenditures benefiting both groups, including maintaining and replacing building envelope components, insurance, and other shared expenses. The commercial group may or may not have its own association. The residential condominium group typically has its own association and fund for components and expenses, such as elevators, hallways, et cetera, benefiting only the condominium owners.

Chapter Takeaways

- All owners pay dues to their own association and a share of the dues to the master for common areas designated for all.
- A master association may or may not include residential units. It may, however, have common property that it maintains.

26

Cohousing and Intentional Communities

A s defined by the Fellowship for Intentional Community, intentional communities "include ecovillages, co-housing, residential land trusts, income-sharing communes, student co-ops, spiritual communities, and other projects where people live together on the basis of explicit common values."[1]

Cohousing originated in Denmark, and in the United States it goes back to the 1980s. The communities range in size, averaging twenty to forty homes. The homes may be attached or single-family, with a general physical design around open space, courtyards, a playground, and, perhaps most important, a common house.

The common house is the heart of the community, and communities may serve one or more optional group meals a week. The design is that the homeowners will form an intentional community, and both casual and intentional meetings with one another will occur.

In the United States, intentional communities and cohousing communities generally take the same form as condominium and single-family home association communities. The major difference in these communities as compared with most other associations is the unique verbiage in the governing documents. Intentional and cohousing communities normally state shared values in the governing documents and have provisions for making decisions via consensus instead of allowing a board of directors to make decisions on the members' behalf. The governing documents may also include provisions for shared meal times and shared responsibilities.

These communities represent a departure from the vast majority of community associations and may be a wonderful experience for members with shared values.

Chapter Takeaways

- There are diverse ways that housing may be owned beyond the normal concepts of condominium, co-op, and planned unit developments.
- While each form of residential housing has a focus or series of focuses, much of that is on building and sustaining a community identity and spirit.
- Screening of future buyers in one form or another may occur in the alternative forms of residential ownership. While much of the screening is done by the community, buyers would be well advised to also screen the community to determine if is a place in which they wish to make a long-term commitment.

27

Assembling the Professional Team When Purchasing a Home within a Community Association

When setting out to purchase a home within a community association, the buyer should give thought to assembling a team of professionals to assist in the search and decision process. Although it is possible for buyers to perform a certain number of the duties mentioned in this chapter themselves, I believe it is wise to rely on professionals knowledgeable in the industry as well.

The following are typical industry professionals included in your team and qualifications to look for when choosing your team:

Real Estate Agent

The real estate agent should not only have experience in representing buyers and sellers but also have a broad knowledge of condominiums and homeowners associations.

Agents are normally licensed by the state, and while their training includes legal concepts, they do not practice law. This includes not being able to provide opinions as to the meaning of CC&Rs and to the legality of actions by a board of directors. Additionally, unless licensed separately, they are not trained in accounting.

Over the last several decades, the concept of the buyers' agent has spread, and many, if not all, states now recognize that a real estate agent may be working for and on behalf of the buyer. Previously, all agents were considered to be working for the seller. As a buyer, working with a sellers' agent is a bit akin to working with the opposing attorney in a lawsuit.

Just because an agent has been involved in the real estate industry for years and has participated in the buying and selling of condominiums does not mean he or she is the best agent to help make the best decision. Do your due diligence and interview prospective real estate agents to ascertain each one's level of experience and understanding when it comes to condominium associations. The best-case scenario is when the real estate agent has a deep understanding of the concepts discussed in this book. The worst-case scenario is when you ask for a copy of the reserve study and the agent asks what it is and why you need it. Make sure you and your real estate agent are on the same page.

Home Inspector

A competent home inspector can be very helpful not only in giving you valuable information on the condition of your unit but also in giving you information on the condition of the buildings and amenities within the association. Many states require a home inspector to be licensed as a contractor.

Do not simply hire a home inspector recommended by the real estate agent or the mortgage broker. Ask the home inspector about his or her experience working with condominiums. Ask the inspector if he or she will include a walkthrough of the entire project and verbally comment on the condition of the buildings, common area property, and amenities, such as swimming pools, clubhouses, and tennis courts. Take good notes on this walkthrough. Compare his or her concerns with the information in the reserve study discussed in chapter 16.

Note, however, that if the condominium is a high-rise, the inspector is unlikely to do much more than a survey of the exterior from the ground and will not do what is called "destructive testing," which is going behind the sheathing material, or "skin," of the building to look for dry rot or other structural issues.

Mortgage Broker

A competent mortgage broker who understands that you need time to analyze documents will be willing to work with you to set realistic deadlines for closing. You do not want to work with a disorganized broker who waits until the last minute to give you closing costs and tries to rush you through closing. I recommend obtaining references from several customers before accepting a referral to a mortgage broker.

Also, while the mortgage broker needs to be willing to provide you the time you need to analyze documents, it is the real estate agent who drafts the contract. The time needed for you to review documents has to be in the contract terms of the offer when it is first written.

Condominium Association Consultant

Once you have reviewed all the documents, a competent condominium association consultant is a valuable resource to help you answer any questions. Unfortunately, there are few individuals that have a multidisciplinary background to advise on all subject areas. Schwindt & Co. is one of the few consultants with this background and is available to assist with understanding and explaining concerns.

Chapter Takeaways

- Real estate agents are trained in the legal aspects of buying and selling real estate but are not trained to interpret legal documents, nor are they allowed to.
- Real estate agents may work on behalf of the buyer, not the seller, in most, if not all, states.
- Mortgage brokers are trained in finance and may need documentation that the condo has met certain federal minimums in budgeting and reserves. They are not trained in the adequacy of budgets and reserves.
- Many, if not most, states may require home inspectors to be contractors. However, home inspectors do not do destructive testing. They are not capable of telling you if there is hidden dry rot or other structural issues that are not immediately visible.

Tips—Best Practices

- Meet with your chosen mortgage broker before looking at property. Have that person do all work possible to have you approved for your loan. Have the documents reviewed by an underwriter. Too many sales get hung up during the lending process for "just one more document."
- Pick a buyers' agent and stick with that person. Some sellers' agents have been known to make all sorts unsubstantiated of statements concerning properties they are selling.

28

The Offer and Documents to Request

When making an offer to purchase a condominium, the buyer should rely on the qualified realtor to submit the legal offer. Offers have certain contingencies written as integral parts of the offer and earnest money agreement. Normally all offers are contingent upon an inspection of the unit by a qualified home inspector. Your realtor may recommend other contingent language.

The offer should also contain the following language (or similar), as recommended by your realtor:

This offer should be contingent upon buyer's review and acceptance of the following documents:

- Declaration and bylaws (CC&Rs)
- Rules and regulations
- Minutes of the board of directors and committee meetings for the past twelve months

- Reserve study (full study including verbiage on condition of components)
- Maintenance plan [mainly to see if there is one]
- Operating budget for the current year
- Internal financial statements (prior year and year-to-date balance sheet and budget-to-actual variance report)
- Audited or reviewed financial statement prepared by a CPA
- Most recent tax return [mainly to ascertain tax returns are being filed]
- List of delinquent homeowner assessments, if available (assessments receivable report)
- List of bills payable (accounts payable report)
- Inspection reports and condition assessment report by architect or engineer
- Seller disclosure statement [if required]
- Answers to various legal, operational, and financial questions

Consider with your agent the possibility of having a timeline for the receipt of the documents and an additional timeline in which to review the documents, to start when you have received the last of them. By separating the information request into two time periods, you avoid having some critical documents come in a day or two before the deadline for approval, thus not leaving you sufficient time to review.

As a purchaser, you are allowed to request these documents from the seller. The seller, as a member of the association, should have the ability to request the documents from the association and answer questions. Please be aware that you may have to pay copy and handling charges to obtain the requested information. Pay them. Knowing whether or not you are taking the turnoff to condo hell is well worth these charges.

Chapter 29 discusses how to analyze information and steps to take when you see possible issues.

Chapter Takeaways

Buyers: Have all terms set out in the original offer, including inspections of documents and approval of them, with sufficient time built in to obtain and review the documents. Sellers want units to sell and want to be "off market" for as little time as possible. Beware of a counteroffer that rushes the timelines.

Tips—Best Practices

- Remember, do as much as possible with your mortgage broker to have all possible processing done before making an offer. A good buyers' agent uses this to strengthen your offer.
- If possible, ask if your agent can start gathering documents on the prospective unit before the offer is presented; if the seller won't provide them, have your agent try to tie down how long it will take to obtain them. This helps in setting the timeline to receive them.

29

Analyzing Information

Once information is received from the seller, it is time to review and analyze the documents and information.

This can be a very subjective process. For example, a buyer who does not own a pet may have no concerns about a pet policy, whereas a buyer with a beloved pet would have a major problem with pet restrictions. For this reason, I strongly suggest that purchasers do not consider hiring consultants who may have a standard score of the association based on predetermined criteria. It is crucial for buyers to understand the concepts explored in this book and apply the information to their particular set of circumstances.

It may be necessary to consult with a professional on specific aspects of the association. This chapter indicates when it may be necessary to consult with a professional. It may also be desirable to consult with an expert after performing a preliminary assessment and obtaining all documents to ensure an unbiased opinion. Such an expert should be well versed in financial, tax, operational, and reserve issues.

Analysis Matrix

Document	Search For (Look for items that are present and those that are missing)	List Buyer Concerns	List Additional Questions to Ask Seller, Association, Inspector, Contractor, Etc.	Response from Seller, Association, Inspector, Contractor, Etc.	Major Issue Yes/No	Amend Offer Yes/No
Declaration of Covenants, Conditions, and Restrictions (CC&Rs) & Bylaws	Restrictions on age, children, pets, renters, smoking, parking, etc. Responsibility for maintenance, repair, or replacement of decks, windows, driveways, sidewalks, fences, painting, etc. Unusual operating provisions: Requirement for annual audit, review, or compilation by a CPA (ask for copy); board members paid for service; board approves special assessments; etc.					
Property Inspection Report	Condition of property for which maintenance, repair, and replacement is the responsibility of owner; maintenance issues that have been deferred					
Complete Building Envelope Inspection Report	Major structural or maintenance issues					
Rules and Regulations	Rules that you cannot accept now (do not expect to change the rules once you are an owner)					

Document	Search For (Look for items that are present and those that are missing)	List Buyer Concerns	List Additional Questions to Ask Seller, Association, Inspector, Contractor, Etc.	Response from Seller, Association, Inspector, Contractor, Etc.	Major Issue Yes/No	Amend Offer Yes/No
Minutes of the Board of Directors Meetings and Committee Meetings	Litigation, operating budget shortfall, construction defects, underfunding of reserves, borrowing from reserves, borrowing from bank, "drama" among members, potential rule enactment, past-due assessments, repair and replacement projects over budget, votes to not follow reserve study's recommended contribution. inconsistencies with what buyer has read in other documents, etc.					
Maintenance Plan	Maintenance plan for major structural and expensive maintenance issues					
Reserve Study	Up-to-date reserve study, cash flow schedule that provides for a positive cash balance every year for the next thirty years, ending balance in reserve study cash flow schedule that matches replacement reserve cash on year-end balance sheet, comments relating to deterioration of common elements (components), construction defects mentioned in description of condition of components, includes all major components (compare to those listed in CC&Rs and bylaws), ensure the reserve study recommends a complete building envelope inspection					

(Continued)

Analysis Matrix (Continued)

Document	Search For (Look for items that are present and those that are missing)	List Buyer Concerns	List Additional Questions to Ask Seller, Association, Inspector, Contractor, Etc.	Response from Seller, Association, Inspector, Contractor, Etc.	Major Issue Yes/No	Amend Offer Yes/No
Budget	Budgeted reserve contributions agree with amount recommended in reserve study (compare to reserve study), large legal fee budget, large bad debt, large maintenance					
Internal Financial Statements	Absence of replacement reserve fund on financial statements **Balance sheet:** No cash in operating and/ or replacement reserve fund, large amount of receivables from owners, interfold balance (amount borrowed from reserves to pay for operating expenses), risky investments (stocks, uninsured deposits), large accounts payable balance, loans from banks, negative fund balances **Statement of Revenues and Expenses:** Special assessments, bad debt expense, large amounts for maintenance, large legal expenses, consultant expenses (need to ask why)					
Audited, Reviewed, or Compiled Financial Statements from a CPA	Refer to search list for internal financial statements. In addition, read the opinion paragraph for an indication of problems with the accuracy of information provided for the audit, review, or compilation. Read notes to the financial statements for indications of issues with the financial health of the association.					

Document	Search For (Look for items that are present and those that are missing)	List Buyer Concerns	List Additional Questions to Ask Seller, Association, Inspector, Contractor, Etc.	Response from Seller, Association, Inspector, Contractor, Etc.	Major Issue Yes/No	Amend Offer Yes/No
Communication with Management and Those Charged with Governance or Management Letter	Does letter written to the board of directors from the CPA suggest certain internal control modifications or noncompliance with the association's governing documents, state or federal statues or laws? Look for major issues.					
Latest Tax Return	Are tax returns filed as required?					
Seller Disclosure Report	Pending special assessments, litigation, noncompliance with local and state statutes, etc.					

The chart included in this chapter may be used to check off documents that have been reviewed, to track questions asked and answers received, and to help you in your buying decision.

When the analysis is complete, review the "Major Issues" column for any marked yeses. Based on any major issues, should you amend the offer?

30

The Decision of Buying or Staying within an Association

To recap, the eventual decision to buy the condominium or single-family residence is based on multiple criteria. These criteria will be different for each buyer. Certain issues, such as rules relating to pets and parking, often fall under the category of whether or not the buyer can live with the restriction. Other issues, such as underfunding reserves or a pending special assessment, can be addressed by amending the purchase offer to compensate for an eventual cash outlay.

In certain cases, this analysis may lead to the conclusion that there are too many concerns, and the best course of action should be to rescind the purchase offer.

I strongly suggest that buyers make use of the Analysis Matrix located in the previous chapter and consider consulting with condominium experts to clarify any issues or to seek a second opinion on any conclusions reached. Schwindt & Co. is available to assist with clarifying issues.

Epilogue

Homeowners associations represent an opportunity for residents to develop a sense of community and a network of support that may not be prevalent in nonassociation communities. In my many years of working with all sizes of associations, I have found that the associations that strive to adhere to best practices in management, finance, and governance have a consistent level of satisfaction among the members and produce a superior level of quality of life for members.

Education, transparency, and communication are the keys for effective community association leadership. It is my fervent hope that this book helps potential purchasers and existing members of associations understand the concepts of best practices of associations and use best efforts to apply these concepts.

The preceding chapters were an overview of important concepts relating to buying and selling, governance, best practices, and creating community within community associations. The following appendices can be used as a tool to expand your knowledge of subjects covered in the preceding chapters.

As I mentioned in the opening chapter, after thirty years of working with community associations, I am still learning new concepts and tools to assist communities in improving governance and community. There are numerous publications that can be used to further your knowledge of the specific concepts discussed in this book, and I encourage you to become a lifelong learner of best practices and share these ideas with your friends and neighbors to help create and sustain vibrant, supportive, and financially sound communities.

For periodic updates and assistance with answering questions relating to the content found in *The Condo Book*, please visit Schwindtco .com. We look forward to being of assistance.

Acknowledgments

I'd like to thank the team of professionals at Schwindt & Co., including Sarah Lane, Diana Chung, Jason Wong, Tim Moore, Carrie Elgin, Yang Thao, Leslie Peters, Timberly Robinson, Michael Weaver, Keith Macomber, and Matt Moeller.

Appendices:
Advanced and Supporting Topics*

---

*All appendices materials are for discussion purposes only. All legal resolutions should be approved by an association's legal counsel.

Appendix A:
Financial Concepts

Contents

Introduction

Appendix A is intended to provide you with a quick, handy reference to many financial issues facing homeowners associations. Appendix A is organized in accordance with the accounting cycle, which consists of approving a budget, billing regular assessments, collecting regular assessments, paying vendor bills, and periodically reporting on finances.

Many sections include easy-to-follow procedures that can be implemented by virtually any association in carrying out its daily operations. There are also other issues discussed, such as accounting for special assessments, borrowing funds from the replacement reserve account, and considering working capital in preparing an annual budget.

Section 1: Duties and Role of the Association Treasurer

Most bylaws outline the duties of the treasurer. Please refer to your bylaws and familiarize yourself with the duties of your association. These duties include:

- Keeping and maintaining a complete set of financial records
- Depositing funds in the name of the association in board-approved depositories
- Overseeing payment of all bills, including proper expense classification
- Identifying, implementing, and monitoring internal controls
- Overseeing an annual compilation, review, or audit by a CPA
- Overseeing insurance coverage
- Overseeing investment of funds
- Billing assessments and collecting delinquent accounts

- Overseeing the replacement reserve program
- Filing all federal, state, and local tax returns in a timely manner
- Reviewing monthly financial statements
- Reviewing monthly bank reconciliations
- Interviewing major contractors
- Communicating financial information to the board and, if appropriate, the membership
- Implementing and monitoring safeguards to protect the association's assets
- Preparing and implementing the operation and reserve budgets
- Monitoring the annual preparation of financial statements by an independent CPA, as well as preparing year-end tax returns, including other appropriate tax and corporate filings
- Working with an outside CPA to evaluate the system of internal controls

Understanding Financial Statements

The Balance Sheet

The balance sheet reflects the association's financial position at a point in time. In essence, it tells the membership what assets they have title to and who owns the assets. The balance sheet is divided into three major categories: assets, liabilities, and members' equity (fund balances), which are segregated into two categories—operating fund and replacement fund. It is called a balance sheet because it is based on a balancing equation: assets equal liabilities plus members' equity. For example:

Assets = liabilities + members' equity

OR

Total assets = what others own + what members own

Assets

Assets represent what the association owns. Common asset categories include: cash (operating and savings), investments, assessments receivable, prepaid insurance, and fixed assets (property and equipment minus accumulated depreciation).

Liabilities

Liabilities represent what the association owes to others. Common liability categories include: accounts payable (unpaid balances to vendors), notes payable, and assessments paid in advance.

Members' Equity

Members' equity (fund balance) represents the association's net worth at a point in time: assets (what the association owns) less liabilities (what the association owes to others) equals members' equity (fund balances).

- **Working capital:** This represents funds collected at settlement from buyers into a community. Usually the equivalent of two months' assessments is collected. The association should refer to the CC&Rs to determine if these amounts can be used solely for operating, unbudgeted, or unusual expenses or if they can be eventually transferred to reserves. In addition, the association's governing documents may provide that working capital contributions be made at the subsequent sale of each unit or that the working capital fund remain at or above a given threshold.
- **Statement of revenues and expenses:** The statement of revenues and expenses summarizes income and expense categories and shows revenues over (under) expenses for the year.

- **Statement of members' equity (fund balance):** This reflects the changes during the year in the association's equity accounts (affected by net revenues over [under] expenses and contributed working capital).

Reports Typically Provided to the Board

Typical reports received by the board include:

- Balance sheet
- Statement of revenues and expenses by class (operating and reserve)
- Cash receipts and cash disbursements
- Assessments receivable aging report
- General ledger detail
- Accounts payable aging report
- Bank statements and bank reconciliations
- Budget-to-actual comparison of revenues and expenses by class

The Treasurer as an Accountant to the Community

In smaller, self-managed communities, the treasurer's function is broadened to include bookkeeping. The treasurer should provide financial reports to the board a few days before the monthly meeting and should give a presentation of the association's financial status at the meeting. See sections 9 to 15 for a discussion of accounting procedures.

Pitfalls to Avoid as Treasurer

Do *not* bring your own agenda to the job of treasurer. Some common personal agendas include:

- Keeping dues at a predetermined level
- Hiring personal friends to perform accounting functions
- Catering to a rival faction

Do not try to keep operating and reserve assessments at a predetermined level. As mentioned in other sections of this manual, the operating and reserve budget process should be conducted without regard to its eventual financial outcome. The numbers are the numbers. Think of yourself as merely a messenger of the amounts that are realistic and meet the objectives of sound financial management.

Keep an open set of books and records. Most associations allow members to inspect financial records. Communicate as often and in as detailed a manner as you can to the membership regarding budgets, variances, cash shortfalls, et cetera. Do *not* hide any financial affairs of the association.

The treasurer and board should be part of the following financial decisions:

- Selecting an accounting method (cash or accrual)
- Selecting a CPA
- Determining whether to perform a compilation, review, or audit
- Determining which tax form to file: 1120 or 1120-H
- Selecting a reserve study provider
- Selecting a banker

Do not use financial service providers unless they are experts at providing services to community associations, are members of appropriate trade organizations (such as the Community Associations Institute), and have a proven track record of providing excellent services to associations. Do not select service providers on the basis of cost alone. You should consider interviewing potential service providers to ensure that they meet the qualifications set by the board.

Although board members are not required to be experts in various aspects of homeowners associations, directors are expected to make sound business decisions by hiring experienced professionals. They should also work with professionals who have the ability to explain complex issues in terms that can be understood by laypersons.

Section 2: Internal Control Considerations

General Information

The board of directors is responsible for safeguarding the association's assets. As such, the association should implement and monitor internal control policies and procedures that help protect the association's assets. Internal controls are procedures implemented by management that ensure the proper recording, summarization, and reporting of financial information, and the safeguarding of the association's assets. The following information outlines recommended internal control practices for condominium and homeowners associations.

Segregation of Duties

The segregation of duties is one of the most effective internal controls in combating fraud and embezzlement. The association's system of checks and balances should include the segregation of duties in each of the association's accounting processes, including cash receipts, accounts receivable, cash disbursements, payroll, inventory, fixed assets, investments, loans, and the financial statement closing process.

Ideally, no individual person should handle more than one of the following duties in a single process: custody of assets, record keeping, authorization, and reconciliation. The association should separate these functions among employee and management personnel. Often, smaller, self-managed associations do not have enough employees or management personnel to segregate all duties. In this case, compensating controls should be put into place. An independent management-level person, who does not have custody, record keeping, authorization, or reconciliation responsibilities, should regularly review and analyze reports and investigate any discrepancies found between reported activity and expectations.

If the association uses a community management company, the board is responsible for understanding and ensuring that the management company's internal controls are adequate and are being followed by the management company.

Cash

Bank Reconciliations

The association should perform reconciliations on all the bank accounts at least monthly to compare bank account activity per the bank statement to bank account activity per the association's records. Timely bank reconciliations allow for discrepancies to be cleared up promptly and with relative ease. All monthly bank reconciliations should be examined and approved by a designated board member. *If the association currently uses or is considering using online banking, please read about online banking, cyber theft, and internal controls in chapter 20.* Consider applying the following procedures in maintaining control over cash.

One of the easiest and most cost-effective safeguards against fraud and embezzlement for homeowners associations is for the board of directors to review bank reconciliations. Here are some tips to consider in reviewing bank reconciliations:

1. Each month, the board of directors or, at a minimum, the treasurer of the board of directors should review the bank reconciliations for all accounts in conjunction with the financial statement review.

2. Each bank reconciliation should include the following information:
   a) The ending balance from the prior month's bank statement.
   b) All transactions that cleared the bank during the month reconciling to the ending balance on the current month's bank statement.
   c) All outstanding items (transactions that have occurred but have not yet cleared the bank) reconciling the ending balance on the bank statement to the ending balance on the financial statements.
   d) The bank statement should be attached to the reconciliation.
      Verify that all checks are accounted for on the reconciliation (no check numbers missing), including voided checks. The list should include the date, check number, payee, and amount of the check. This list should be reviewed for reasonableness and examined for duplicate payments and old outstanding checks.

3. Verify that all deposits are included in the reconciliation. Examine the outstanding items for old outstanding deposits.

4. Make sure that all transfers between accounts are reflected on both account reconciliations in the same period. All transfers listed should indicate which account received the transfer and the purpose of the transfer.

5. Ask for more information if any item comes to your attention that seems to be out of the ordinary.

6. Review and approval of the bank reconciliations should be documented in the board of directors' meeting minutes.

Dual Signatures

The association should institute a dual-signature policy that requires two authorized signatures on all cash disbursements over a certain prescribed dollar amount ($1,000 is recommended).

Maintaining and Updating Authorized Check Signers

As board terms are limited, so too is authorized check signing authority. Authorizing signature cards should be updated and reviewed on an annual basis to remove signers who are no longer authorized. Obtain the authorizing signature cards from the association's financial institution. Most financial institutions can assist with completing the necessary paperwork.

Cash Receipts

All incoming checks should be restrictively endorsed "For Deposit Only" by the individual opening the mail or receiving the check. Cash and check receipts should be stored in a safe or locked cabinet until the time of bank deposit. Deposits should be made on a daily basis.

Voided Checks

Voided checks should be properly disposed of with the signature section removed.

Investment Policy

The association should develop and implement an investment policy that addresses uninsured deposits. Bank deposits are insured by the Federal Deposit Insurance Corporation (FDIC) up to $250,000 at any one financial institution. If the association has uninsured deposits, the association could consider moving some funds to the Certificate of Deposit Account Registry Service (CDARS). CDARS offers a convenient way to obtain full FDIC insurance on deposit amounts larger than $250,000 by breaking large deposits into smaller amounts and placing them with other banks that are members of its special network. If the association has certificates of deposit (CDs) with another financial institution (for example, with a brokerage company), care needs to be taken that they are adequately insured as they may not be covered by the FDIC.

Competitive Bidding Policy

The association should consider establishing a formal competitive bidding policy, whereby a certain number of bids and other parameters are established for the solicitation of bids for major projects. Lack of competitive bidding may result in overpayment of time and materials.

Other

- Avoid signing blank checks
- Store blank checks in a locked cabinet
- Pay vendor bills only from an original invoice, never from a duplicate or fax

Assessments Receivable

Periodic Examination of Past-Due Assessments

The board of directors should be provided with a monthly delinquency report for examination and approval. Additional information should be requested for anything that appears out of the ordinary. In addition, collection efforts should be examined for each delinquency. Potentially uncollectible amounts should be considered classified as potential bad debt with a corresponding allowance for doubtful accounts.

Late Fee and Collection Policy

The association should consider establishing a formal late fee and collection policy that provides for the treatment of late assessments—including interest on late payments, number of days until account is liened or turned over for collections, et cetera. This policy should be adopted by a board resolution.

Bad Debts

Delinquent assessments receivable should be analyzed to determine collectability. Liens should be placed on all accounts that are more than ninety days past due.

If the books and records are on the accrual method of accounting, the board should consider recording a bad debt and a corresponding allowance for doubtful accounts for assessments that are in danger of not being collected. Care should be taken not to completely write off receivables by taking the amounts off the accounting records, even if foreclosure occurs and the homeowner is no longer a member of the association. It is possible to eventually receive payment if the former member wishes to clear his or her credit history by paying on past-due amounts. The treasurer should consult with appropriate experts, such as CPAs and collection attorneys, for guidance.

Fixed Assets

General Information

Capitalized assets are depreciated over their estimated useful lives in accordance with the association's formally adopted fixed-asset capitalization policy. Elements of a good capitalization policy follow.

Capitalization Policy for Association-Purchased Assets

Capitalization is the recognition on the balance sheet of the association's property and equipment. The capitalization policy sets guidelines regarding what assets are appropriate for capitalization and at what dollar amount the assets should be capitalized. The elements of a good capitalization policy are as follows:

1. There is a clear understanding of what is appropriate for capitalization.
   a) For condominium associations, real property and common areas acquired from the developer and related improvements to such property are not capitalized because those properties generally are owned by the individual unit owners in common and not by the association.
   b) For homeowners associations, real property and common areas acquired by the original homeowners from the developer are generally not capitalized on the association's financial statements. Real property and common areas are defined as common areas in the association's governing documents. Real property taxes are paid by the association members on a pro rata basis on this type of real property. Although these properties are owned by the association, the assets are not normally recognized under generally accepted accounting principles due to the fact that the association will not, in the ordinary course of business, dispose of the property to generate significant cash flows.
2. An association may hold title to common personal property. Generally accepted accounting principles require associations to capitalize common personal property, such as furnishings,

recreational and maintenance equipment, and work vehicles. Associations hold title to personal property, and the association's board of directors is able to sell personal property at its discretion; the association retains the proceeds. Thus, the property qualifies for asset recognition.

3. An association may hold title to real property that is not included as common areas in the governing documents. Property taxes are paid by the association on this type of real property. The association's board of directors has the ability to sell this property, and the association retains the proceeds. Thus, the property qualifies for asset recognition.

4. Property that should be considered for capitalization are those assets having the following criteria:

   a) The association has clear title or other evidence of ownership.

   b) The association can dispose of the property for cash.

   c) The property is used by the association to generate cash from nonmember sources.

   d) The association has the title to real property that can be sold.

5. A dollar limitation based on the asset's cost basis should be imposed on depreciable capitalized items. The amount of limitation depends on the size of the association. Reasonable levels might range from $1,000 to $5,000. Items below this dollar limitation are then expensed and not capitalized.

6. Property that is capitalized should be presented in the operating fund (or in a separate fund established for that purpose) and depreciated over the estimated useful life of the asset on a straight-line basis

Section 3: Accounting Software

Selecting the right accounting software can seem overwhelming, as there are many accounting software programs available for purchase. However, selecting an accounting software package can be simplified greatly if you know what features to look for. In selecting accounting software for common interest realty associations, the software should contain the following modules:

- Banking
- Invoicing
- Bill paying
- Budgeting
- Payroll processing

Additionally, the accounting software should serve as a management tool by providing reports, such as budget-to-actual comparisons, aging reports, and other financial reports. The software should be user friendly and easy to learn.

Section 4: Accounting Users and Passwords

To ensure the integrity of the association's financial records, authorized users of the association's bookkeeping software should be minimized. Each user should always log in under a unique username and password. A new password should be created when there is a turnover in personnel.

The following need to be authorized users in the association's accounting software:

- Administrator—IT
- Manager
- Accountant

Section 5: Chart of Accounts

The chart of accounts is a listing of all accounts in an association's general ledger. The following is a list of the most frequently used accounts in an association's chart of accounts and includes a description of each account. It is recommended that a designated board member approve all future changes to the chart of accounts. An example chart of accounts can be found in appendix D.

Assets

Checking and Savings Accounts

- **Operating bank accounts:** These accounts contain the funds designated for paying operating expenses. All assessments collected from homeowners, including operating and reserve assessments, are deposited into the operating checking account.
- **Payroll account:** This account contains the funds designated for payroll expenses, including wages and applicable payroll taxes. Funds are transferred to this account monthly from the operating bank account.
- **Replacement reserve bank accounts:** These accounts contain the funds designated to pay replacement fund expenses. Every month, the association transfers the monthly reserve assessments from the operating fund to the reserve fund.
- **Special assessment bank accounts:** These accounts contain the funds designated for special assessment projects. When a special assessment is collected from a homeowner, it is typically deposited directly into these accounts. However, a homeowner may write one check that includes the regular operating assessments and the special assessment. When this occurs, the check is deposited into the operating fund, and the treasurer then transfers the special assessment portion to the appropriate bank account.

Other Assets

- **Interfund balance:** These accounts are used to track the amounts borrowed and payable among the operating, reserve, and other fund accounts. An interfund balance arises when one fund pays amounts that are proper expenses of another fund. An interfund balance may also arise when a budgeted transfer has not been made, including the transfer of the monthly reserve assessments from the operating fund. Ideally, the balance in these accounts should be zero at the end of each month after the treasurer has made the appropriate transfers for the month.

- **Assessments receivable (accrual basis):** These accounts contain amounts billed to the owners for all assessments. More than one assessment receivable account may be used if owners are billed separately for reserve assessments and special assessments.

- **Prepaid expenses (accrual basis):** These accounts contain amounts paid for expenses pertaining to a future reporting period, such as an insurance payment made for the entire year.

- **Fixed assets (accrual basis):** These accounts contain the cost basis amount for capitalized assets.

- **Accumulated depreciation (accrual basis):** This account contains the total depreciation on fixed assets currently on the association's balance sheet.

Liabilities

- **Accounts payable (accrual basis):** This account contains amounts owed by the association for expenses accrued during the current period.

- **Prepaid assessments (accrual basis):** This account contains the amount of assessments paid by owners that is not due until a subsequent reporting period.
- **Note payable:** This account contains the principal balance on a note or loan payable by the association.

Members' Equity (Fund Balance)

- **Members' equity—operating (operating fund balance):** This account contains the accumulated earnings of the operating fund to date. The current year's accumulated income and loss may be a separate line item that, when added to the prior year's accumulated earnings, equals total members' equity less operating fund.
- **Members' equity—replacement (replacement fund balance):** This account contains the accumulated earnings of the replacement fund to date. The current year's accumulated income and loss may be a separate line item which, when added to the prior year's accumulated earnings, equals total members' equity less replacement fund.
- **Members' equity—working capital (working capital fund balance):** Certain association's governing documents require that a separate fund for working capital be maintained. This account contains the accumulated earnings of the working capital fund to date. The current year's accumulated income and loss may be a separate line item that, when added to the prior year's accumulated earnings, equals total members' equity less replacement fund.
- **Working capital contributions:** This account contains the amount of working capital contributed to the working capital fund, which is based on requirements in the association's governing documents.

Revenue

- **Assessments—operating:** This account details the amount of assessments billed, which is based on budgeted assessments if the association is on the accrual basis. Associations reporting on the cash basis show actual assessments collected.
- **Assessments—replacement:** This account details the amount of assessments billed for replacement assessments if the association is on the accrual basis or the amount of contribution if the association is on the cash method.
- **Interest—operating:** This account details the amount of interest earned or collected on interest-bearing operating bank accounts.
- **Interest—replacement:** This account details the amount of interest earned on interest-bearing replacement bank accounts.
- **Interest—working capital:** This account details the amount of interest earned on interest-bearing working capital bank accounts.
- **Other revenue accounts:** Accounts should be created according to the association's needs. Each budget item should have a separate revenue account to assist the board in analyzing budget-to-actual comparisons and in developing the subsequent year's budget.

Expenses

- **Operating expense accounts:** Accounts should be created according to the association's needs. Each budget line item should have a separate expense account to assist the board in analyzing budget-to-actual comparisons and in developing the subsequent year's budget.

- **Replacement expense accounts:** These accounts contain the details of major repairs and replacement expenses. The reserve study, and thus the replacement fund budget, should be used as guidance in determining the expenses that should be coded to these accounts. The association may want to use only one expense account, or it may want to keep one expense account for each component.

Other Revenue and Expenses

At times, the association may levy special assessments to pay for a designated expenditure, or it may receive proceeds from a legal settlement. Activity related to special assessments or litigation proceeds that are designated for a specific expenditure should be tracked in separate revenue and expense accounts, and depending on the nature of the activity, the association may want to track this in funds other than operating or replacement reserves. Separate general ledger accounts should be created for the revenue and expenses related to each fund.

Section 6: Annual Budget

General Information

Annually, the association should prepare and adopt an operating and reserve budget for the ensuing fiscal year. This annual budget is the basis for establishing annual regular member assessments to cover operating expenses and contributions to the replacement reserve fund. The annual budget is a financial action plan, and it should be realistic.

To prepare an operating and reserve budget each year, the association will need to prepare the following budgets:

- **Operating budget:** The operating budget is based on estimated expenses required for the ongoing upkeep and maintenance of the association, such as utilities, payroll, general maintenance, et cetera. It is also prudent to factor in a contingency or emergency budget line item of around 5 to 10 percent of all other operating expenses for unexpected operating costs. The operating budget should also include a line item for bad debts (see section 7 for a discussion of bad debts). Each operating budget line item should be supported by a written narrative explaining in detail how the amount was computed.

- **Reserve budget:** The association's reserve budget should be based on its reserve study. The reserve study should be updated each year. Most associations are required by statute to prepare and annually update a reserve study (see section 8 for more).

Section 7: Accounting for Bad Debts

Collection of assessments is a major problem for many associations. This issue affects the association's ability to qualify for loans, to satisfy HUD requirements to become approved for FHA loans, and, of course, to fund ongoing cash flow needs. This section offers ways to assist associations in the collection process and also discusses the appropriate accounting treatment of allowing for and writing off uncollectible assessments.

Associations should receive and review a listing of past-due assessments monthly, which details the name of the member, the amount due, and the past-due period segregated by 30, 60, 90, and 120 days or more past due. Past-due homeowner assessments in many states are automatically liened. If the unit is voluntarily sold, the full amount of the lien must be paid unless the association agrees to a lesser amount. If title passes and the lien is not paid in full, the lien passes to the new owner. If the unit is involuntarily sold through foreclosure, there is a danger the lien will not be paid if there are insufficient funds to pay the underlying mortgage. If there are not sufficient funds to pay the mortgage, the association will not recover assessments. Because of this, a lien is also filed (recorded) with the county. This lien is filed by the association's attorney or the firm engaged to provide collection services. This lien will appear on the title report. It is also possible to obtain a judgment personally against the debtor and perform additional collection techniques, such as garnishing wages. Once a judgment is obtained, the lien will appear on the member's credit report.

The series of events that may lead a debt to eventual noncollection is as follows:

- The member fails to pay assessments for an extended period of time. A lien is filed against the member.
- The member does not pay the mortgage on the unit and the financial institution begins foreclosure proceedings.
- The financial institution forecloses on the unit, and there are insufficient funds to pay the mortgage. In this instance, other liened debts of lesser priority, such as unpaid assessments, are extinguished.
- The member files Chapter 7 personal bankruptcy, extinguishing all personal debts including the past due assessment. (In some cases Chapter 13 will extinguish the debt.)

Until the debtor files Chapter 7 or 13 personal bankruptcy, there is a possibility of collection, and collection efforts may recover all or a part of the outstanding debt.

Accounting Treatment

Cash basis financial statements merely recognize revenue when dues are received, regardless of whether the dues are current or delinquent. Because accrual basis financial statements record assessment income when the assessments are due rather than when the dues are actually received, they require the association to record assessments receivable.

If the association believes an assessment is in danger of not being collected, it is appropriate to record a bad debt expense by reducing the receivable balance via an account labeled "allowance for doubtful accounts" and recording a noncash expense line item labeled "bad debt expense." This, in effect, records an expense in the period the association believes the debt becomes in danger of noncollection. It should be noted that this accounting treatment does not take the member's balance off the listing of assessments receivable. It merely reduces the total balance of all receivables by the amount in danger of collection. A debt is in danger of collection warranting a bad debt expense and related allowance for doubtful accounts when foreclosure proceedings have begun. Until this happens, appropriate collection efforts are deemed to render the debt to be reasonably collectible unless there is other evidence to suggest the debt is in danger of noncollection.

When there is no chance of collection, the debt is permanently deleted from the listing of assessments receivable. Deleting the account is called "writing off" the receivable. The distinction between recording an allowance account and writing off the account is important. By recording the allowance, the association is preserving information relating to the past-due account on association records including the listing of assessments receivable.

If the debtor sometime in the future wishes to extinguish the debt and thereby remove the debt from his or her credit report, it may be necessary to verify the debt. If the debt is written off, the association may not have the necessary information to satisfy reporting agencies. Therefore, I recommend that past-due assessments never be written off until the association becomes aware the debtor has gone through personal bankruptcy, thus extinguishing all debts, including amounts owed to the association. This information is communicated to the association by the attorney in charge of collections, indicating the matter is closed and collection activities have ceased.

Bad debts, if recorded correctly, can aid in proper budgeting. Properly prepared budgets should recognize that not all members will pay assessments on time. Therefore, including a bad debt line item in the budget will allow the association to increase required assessments to compensate for uncollected assessments.

By systematically budgeting, accounting, reviewing, placing liens, and employing aggressive assessment collection efforts, associations can help minimize the impact of uncollectable assessments.

Section 8: Preparing a Reserve Study

General Information

Educated buyers are looking closer at an association's reserve funds (or lack thereof) as a basis for determining the purchase price or buying a comparable unit or house with a sound reserve game plan in place.

Many states require reserve funding, including the preparation of a reserve study, for most associations. For those states that do not, it is still best practice to do so.

Reasons to prepare and update a reserve study and follow the funding requirements are as follows:

- Meets the fiduciary responsibility of the board
- Meets statutory requirements
- Meets legal requirements dictated by the CC&Rs
- Provides for planned funding of major expenditures
- Distributes the cost of future expenditures to old and new owners
- Matches the enjoyment and use of facilities to the ratable value
- Minimizes the need for a special assessment, especially if some owners are on fixed incomes and are not able to pay large special assessments
- Enhances resale values
- Is recommended by accounting standards (as are funding reserves, segregating capital vs. noncapital assets, and segregating funds) and may help reduce income taxes for individual owners when a unit is sold
- Meets HUD and Fannie Mae requirements

The association should seek consultation on its financial needs with its property manager, accountant, engineer, et cetera, before proceeding with the study.

Reserve studies should be updated annually. Changes in the estimated current cost to repair, inflation, interest earned on accumulated reserve deposits, and expected life of each item all affect the amount that should be contributed to reserves each year in order to meet the funding needs of the association. If these elements are not considered annually, the association may need to suddenly increase assessments in order to "catch up" to the necessary funding level. Gradual increases in budgeted reserve assessments are preferred over unexpected spikes. The association should consult with the state statutes and the association's governing documents to determine legal requirements.

Treasurers should be aware of various methods used by reserve study professionals to compute the required contribution. Terms such as *full funding*, *percent funded*, *threshold method*, and *baseline method* can be confusing.

All reserve studies should include a cash flow schedule detailing the beginning balance, plus required reserve contribution, plus interest earned, minus expenditures (adjusted for inflation), and ending balance each year. This schedule should show this activity for a thirty-year period. The ending cash balance for each year should never drop below zero. If the ending balance drops below zero, the association will need to special-assess.

The ending balance for each year is the threshold balance. If the ending balance never drops below $50,000 over a thirty-year period, theoretically, the association will always have at least $50,000 to pay for contingencies. This amount of overfunding leads to much discussion in the reserve study industry. The treasurer should consult with the reserve study provider or a CPA to determine the appropriate amount of overfunding (the minimum threshold).

Additional information on reserve funding and a risk mitigation matrix can be found in appendix E.

Section 9: Monthly Accounting and Bookkeeping Tasks

Replacement Reserve Expenditures

If possible, the association should pay its replacement reserve expenditures from the reserve bank account. However, if the operating bank account pays replacement reserve expenditures, the operating bank account should be reimbursed as soon as possible. It should be noted that due to withdrawal restrictions on many money market and investment brokerage accounts, and for practicality reasons, it might be necessary to pay replacement fund expenditures through the operating fund checking account. A detailed record should be kept of each payment made by the operating fund on behalf of the replacement fund and a repayment transfer should be made at least once a month. See the description of interfund balances in section 5 for more.

Bank Transfers

The association should consider authorizing the manager to make certain preauthorized banking transfers to free up board members. I recommend developing a form or template that includes a line for the date, affected bank accounts, transfer amount, purpose, and authorized signatures. The form and transfers should be approved by the board at a regularly scheduled meeting and given to the manager to make the transfers. The following routine bank transfers should be made on a monthly basis:

1. **Reserve contribution (operating to reserve):** The approved budget should be followed in determining the amount to transfer.
2. **Reimburse operating for reserve expenditures:** This occurs when the operating fund pays for reserve expenditures as a matter of convenience.

Reconciling Association Fund Balances

Interfund balances may occur for several reasons. The association should reconcile its fund balances on a monthly basis, including determining outstanding interfund balances among the funds for unreimbursed expenses and transfers. Interfund balances occur when one fund pays the expenses for a second fund without being reimbursed. For example, the association's operating account might pay the replacement reserve expenditures and later be reimbursed by the reserve account. Between the date the operating account pays the reserve expenditures and the date the replacement account reimburses the operating account, there is an interfund balance. Other causes of interfund balances include the following:

1. Budgeted reserve assessments were reported in the reserve fund, but cash was not transferred from the operating cash account to the reserve cash account.
2. The operating fund borrowed from reserves to pay for unanticipated expenses.
3. Expenses for one fund were incorrectly coded to another fund.
4. Operating cash was transferred to reserve cash accounts to earn higher interest.

Bank Reconciliations

The treasurer or manager should reconcile all bank accounts on a monthly basis. The treasurer should focus on the items listed in section 2, on internal control considerations, when performing the monthly bank account reconciliations.

Statements to Delinquent Owners

Monthly statements should be mailed to delinquent owners to serve as reminders. Note: If the delinquent account has been turned over to collections, the attorney will require that no further contact be made between the association and the delinquent owner concerning the debt, as part of the federal Fair Debt Collection Practices Act.

Monthly Replacement Reserve Fund Contributions

The reserve contributions are reported separate from operating assessments in the statement of revenues and expenses and accumulate in a due-from operating/due-to reserve account on the balance sheet until the contributions are actually paid.

Section 10: Billing and Cash Receipts

Assessments

General Information

As stated in section 6, the annual budget is the basis for establishing annual regular member assessments to cover operating expenses and the contribution to the replacement reserve fund. Budgeted regular assessments should be allocated to each member in accordance with the association's legal documents.

Some Tips on Setting Up Owner Accounts

1. The lot or unit number and the owner's name should be used as the owner (customer) name. It may also be helpful to use leading zeros. For example, if there are more than 100 units, use 045 rather than 45. This will be useful when generating reports so that units will be listed in numerical order.
2. If ownership changes or a new account has to be created for an owner, the old account should be renamed in some consistent way to designate that the account has changed. For example: Accounts for old owners might have an additional digit at the end of the unit number (045 vs. 0459) or prebankruptcy balances might have an additional two digits at the end of the unit number (045 vs. 04599).
3. After changing the name of the old account, the new owner's account can be created with the unit number and name of the new owner.
4. On the date the customer information is entered into the bookkeeping system, it is important that the owner's balance to date is entered. Assessments receivable pertaining to prior year's

assessments should be entered using the prior years' billing dates. Assessments receivable pertaining to the current year should be entered using the current year's billing date. This tip applies to existing associations who are changing bookkeeping software or entering information into a system for the first time.

It is also important to update owners' names on a regular basis in order to keep activity for each owner (account) separate.

Accounting Procedures

The following accounting procedures can be used in member billing and cash receipts:

- **Billing:** Once the annual budget is approved, members should be billed accordingly.
- **Cash receipts:** The following accounting procedures should be used related to cash receipts on a daily basis.
  1. Restrictively endorse check immediately. A restrictive endorsement stamp can be ordered through your financial institution.
  2. Prepare a deposit slip that lists all cash, coins, and checks received.
  3. Copy the deposit slip and all checks received.
  4. Post cash receipts to the respective member assessments receivable accounts.
  5. Deliver the deposit to the bank on a daily basis.
  6. Attach the validated deposit slip received from the bank to the cash receipt copy prepared in step 3 and file temporarily in a daily deposit folder until the bank reconciliation is completed for the month.

Section 11: Cash Disbursements

General Information

The association's approved annual budget should indicate what types of operating expenses the association expects to incur during the year. Whether an expense is classified as an operating fund expense or a replacement fund expense is governed by the adoption of the association's annual budget. If the association incurs expenses that have not been budgeted for, they should be reported in the fund that most closely relates to the nature of the expenses and documented by a formal board resolution.

Accounting Procedures

The following accounting procedures can be used for cash disbursements:

1. On a periodic basis (weekly, biweekly, etc.), all vendor bills received should be forwarded to a designated board member for general ledger account coding, proper classification (operating or reserve fund), and approval for payment. The designated signer should initial the approved invoice, indicating that the bill should be paid, along with proper coding.
2. The bills should then be posted and a vendor payment check prepared. It is important to note from which bank account bills are being paid. If the operating fund pays reserve fund expenditure, this creates an amount due from the reserve fund to the operating fund. An entry to record the amount due to operating from replacement should be made in the interfund balance accounts.
3. The payment check, along with the original vendor bill, should be forwarded to the authorized check signer.

4. The authorized check signer, or another designated individual other than the person preparing the payment check, should mail the vendor payments.

5. Attach a copy of the check voucher to the paid vendor bill and file. If voucher checks are not used, a "PAID" stamp should be used, and the date, check number, and initials should be placed directly on the paid vendor bill.

Section 12: Payroll Transactions

If the association has employees, appropriate forms, payments, and other documentation should be completed on a timely basis. See sections 20 and 21 for information regarding association employees.

The association may choose to hire an outside firm to prepare its payroll reports, schedule tax payments, and send paychecks and tax payments on its behalf. A payroll service will prepare monthly journal entries that should be made to the association's books and records.

Payroll expenses, including payroll taxes, may be paid from a payroll bank account, which should be replenished monthly from the operating bank account.

Section 13: Reserve Contributions

General Information

As part of the association's operating and reserve budget, a portion of regular assessments may be used to fund the replacement reserve account. Regular reserve assessments (future major repairs and replacements) should be reported separately from assessments for operations in the period assessed.

Accounting Procedures

When accounts receivable for reserves and operating are both reported in the operating fund, the following accounting procedures should be used in making periodic reserve contributions:

1. On the first day of each month, the association should transfer funds from the operating bank account to the reserve bank account for the monthly reserve contribution.
2. A general journal entry should be made each month to reclassify the reserve contribution from the operating classification to the reserve fund classification. (These entries can be set up in advance for each of twelve monthly transfers.)

In this case, bad debt is reported as an operating expense.

Alternate Accounting Procedures

When accounts receivable operating and accounts receivable reserves are reported in separate funds, the following accounting procedures should be used in making periodic reserve contributions:

1. On the first day of each month, the association should transfer funds from the operating bank account to the replacement bank account for the amount of replacement assessments actually collected.
2. Operating assessments and replacement assessments may be shown as separate line items and posted to the corresponding assessment revenue account at the time of billing. Under this method, replacement assessments receivable will be shown separate from operating assessments receivable.

In this case, bad debt for reserves is reported in the reserve fund. The reserve study should include a contingency for bad debt.

Section 14: Reserve Fund Borrowing and Working Capital

Borrowing from the Reserve Fund

Most states require or provide for associations to reserve funds for future repairs and replacements of common property. Normally those funds are required to be separate from operating funds. Depending on state law or the association's governing documents, the board of directors may borrow from reserve funds to meet high seasonal demands on the operating funds or to meet unexpected increases. Either state law or the association's governing documents may require payback of any loans from reserves; if not, best practice is that the loan is paid back within a reasonable amount of time. An attorney should be consulted prior to making the loan to ensure compliance.

It should be noted that due to withdrawal restrictions on many money market and investment brokerage accounts, and for practicality reasons, it might be necessary to pay replacement fund expenditures through the operating fund checking account. A detailed record should be kept of each payment made by the operating fund on behalf of the replacement reserve fund and a repayment transfer should be made at least once a month. See section 5 for a definition of interfund balance accounts.

Working Capital Considerations

Some associations prefer to keep a certain amount of cash in the operating cash account to absorb seasonal cash flow needs as well as to pay for unforeseen operating expenses. In addition, the association's governing documents may require working capital contributions at the initial sale or at each sale of a unit. This surplus cash is sometimes computed at two to six times the monthly operating budget. If this average cash surplus drops below the desired amount, the budget may be adjusted to help build up this cash surplus to a comfortable level.

If there are many unanticipated expenses occurring, the association may wish to consider adding an amount to the operating and replacement fund budgets for contingency expenses. This is an account that can be used when unbudgeted events occur and for which the association should provide a definition.

Section 15: Special Assessments

General Information

Associations have the authority to levy special assessments. The association should take care in levying special assessments in accordance with governing documents. Special assessments are sometimes levied to fund future major repairs and replacement deficiencies; or, in addition to regular reserve assessments, to offset operating deficits, to provide for unanticipated expenses (such as litigation costs); or to provide for a contingency or emergency fund for other unanticipated expenses.

A board resolution should include the following elements: dollar amount, proposed use of funds, method of allocation among the affected members, member payment terms, and late-fee policy. The proposed use of funds should specify deposit into either the operating fund or the replacement fund and the use as either for general expenses or for a designated expense. This determines into which bank account the collected special assessments should be deposited. If a special assessment is approved for a designated purpose, the revenue and related expenses may be classified in a separate special assessment fund.

The board resolution should be provided to the accounting department or accountant.

Accounting Procedures

The following accounting procedures can be used in accounting for special assessments:

1. A charge should be assessed to each member's assessment receivable account in accordance with the board resolution. It is important to classify these charges as "special assessment fund," "operating fund," or "reserve fund." This information should be stated in the board resolution. If it is not, a board member should be consulted.

2. If requested, generate an invoice for delivery to each member. The invoice should explain the purpose for the special assessment, the late fee policy, the payment terms, et cetera.

3. Special assessment cash collections should be deposited into the designated bank account. If it is necessary to deposit the special assessment cash receipts into a bank account other than that designated, a detailed record should be maintained. The special assessment cash should be transferred to the designated bank account as soon as possible.

4. Late charges should be applied in accordance with the board resolution.

Section 16: Financial Reporting to the Board

Periodic In-House Financial Reporting

General Information

It is important that the board of directors examine the association's financial statements on a periodic basis. A monthly examination is recommended. The board is responsible for the protection of the association's assets. As such, the periodic examination of financial information allows for the timely identification and investigation of potential errors and irregularities that may exist in the association's financial records. In addition, examination of periodic financial information allows the board to compare actual operating results to that budgeted and to investigate and control ensuing budget variances.

Basis of Accounting

Financial reports are prepared on the cash or accrual method or by using a combination of the two methods. Generally accepted accounting principles require the accrual method of accounting. The accrual and cash methods are discussed in more detail below.

- **Accrual method:** The accrual method of accounting reports revenue in the period earned and expenses in the period incurred. Thus, assessment revenue is reported when due rather than when the payment is actually received by the association. The accrual method of accounting is preferred because it facilitates a better comparison of actual operating results to the annual budget. Additionally, the accrual method of accounting reflects a more accurate depiction of the association's financial position than that of the cash method.

- **Cash-basis method:** The cash-basis method of accounting reports revenues and expenses based on the physical cash
inflows and outflows of the association. It is important to
note that the cash method financial reports do not include
delinquent assessments or unpaid vendor bills. It is recommended that the following additional reports be used in conjunction with cash basis reports: assessments receivable aging
report to identify amounts due to the association; accounts
payable report to identify amounts due to vendors for services
rendered.
- **Modified cash-basis method:** This method adds certain components of the accrual method, such as receivables and prepaid
assessments, but leaves out other accrual based accounts, such as
accounts payable.

Accounting Procedures

On a monthly basis (or other basis), the board of directors is given
the following financial reports for review:

1. Balance sheet
2. Statement of revenues and expenses by class (operating and reserve)
3. Budget-to-actual comparison of revenues and expenses by class
   (operating and reserve)
4. Bank reconciliation reports and copies of bank statements for
   the month
5. Accounts receivable aging report
6. Accounts payable aging report
7. General ledger detail report for the month
8. A list of all checks written, sorted by check number (out-
   of-sequence checks should be investigated)

Annual Financial Reporting

General Information

Many associations are subject to annual financial reporting requirements either by governing documents or by state statute. Accountants are engaged to compile, review or audit, and report on the
association's annual financial statements.

Financial Statements

There are three types of assurances CPAs place on financial statements. These assurances in order of reliance are as follows:

- **Compilation:** When a CPA compiles financial statements
  for a client, the CPA presents information obtained from the
  client in the form of financial statements in accordance with
  generally accepted accounting principles. The CPA does not
  audit or review the information and places no assurance on the
  statements. However, if, in the course of this preparation, the
  CPA notices anything peculiar about the information, the CPA
  is required to investigate to satisfy himself or herself that the
  information would not be misleading to a user.
- **Review:** A review consists of compiling the information into
  the form of financial statements prepared in accordance with
  generally accepted accounting principles and applying analytical
  review procedures to the information to provide limited assurance that nothing came to the attention of the CPA that would
  lead him or her to believe the statements were not fairly presented. This analysis includes, but is not be limited to, vouching for balance sheet amounts to supporting documentation
  and comparing current-year revenue and expense amounts to

prior-year and budgeted amounts. This type of assurance is far less than an audit. If the CPA becomes aware of a peculiarity as a result of this review, it is incumbent upon the CPA to perform additional procedures.

- **Audit:** Audited financial statements require the CPA to perform such procedures as promulgated by generally accepted auditing standards to enable the CPA to express an opinion as to the fairness of the financial information. This means the CPA will tell you if he or she believes the amounts reported in the financial statements are materially correct. An audit also requires the CPA to document and analyze the system of internal controls inherent in the accounting system. Any weaknesses in internal controls and other operational efficiency comments are normally communicated via a management letter to the board of directors. See chapter 15 for further discussion on financial audits.

Which Form of Reporting Should You Use?

Associations should require at least a yearly compilation. Most large associations require either a review or an audit at year-end. Factors in requiring a review or audit are frequently:

1. Requirement in state statutes
2. Requirement in association's governing documents
3. Time period elapsed from the last audited report
4. Familiarity with the association's management company and ongoing financial information
5. Change in management companies
6. Turnover from the declarant to the member board of directors
7. Subsequent change in the board of directors

Statutes on Annual Audit, Review, or Compilation of Financial Statements

States vary in their requirements concerning audits, reviews, and compilations. Some, for example, may set a minimum dollar amount before an audit, review, or compilation is required. There may be requirements for associations turned over after a certain date; requirements for a mix of reviews, audits, and compilations; and exceptions made for or against an audit based on an owner vote. Be sure to look to statutes specific to an HOA or condominium and also to other statutes covering nonprofit corporations.

Preparing for Audit, Review, or Compilation

- Fund balances (retained earnings or members' equity) at the beginning of the year should agree with the fund balances as of the end of the prior year. Any adjustments entered in these accounts should be reconciled.
- Accounts payable should have a positive (credit) balance unless payments were made before the end of the year and bills were entered after the end of the year. In that case, the CPA will need this information when performing the audit, review, or compilation.
- Accounts payable aging report balance should agree with the ending general ledger (GL) balance.
- Undeposited cash should only include the balance of cash on hand that has not yet been deposited in the bank by the year-end date. Payments received on assessments should be applied to owner balances when they are entered into the accounting software so the balance will not cause undeposited cash to be misstated.
- Accounts receivable should have a positive (debit) balance unless prepaid assessments were entered in owner's receivable accounts.

In that case, separate reports should be generated to show total of accounts greater than zero (accounts receivable) and total of accounts less than zero (prepaid assessments). Prior to printing these reports, payments received from owners should be credited to the owners' unpaid balances.

- Accounts receivable aging report balance should agree with the ending GL balance.
- Interest on CDs and other cash accounts should be posted prior to sending the GL and financial statements to the CPA. The board should always be able to get reports on CD balances upon request.
- Financial statements and the GL provided for the financial engagement should be printed directly from the accounting software and should all be printed on the same basis of accounting, either accrual basis or cash basis.

Steps in the Audit Process

An understanding of services to be provided will be established with an engagement letter between the association and its CPA. The association's main point of contact should be indicated. The association's desired due date should be communicated.

Information will be requested and should be provided to the CPA in a timely manner in order for the audit process to be completed in time to meet the association's desired due date.

Fieldwork date(s) will be scheduled for evaluating the design and implementation of the entity's internal control system and for obtaining adequate information to form an opinion on the financial statements as a whole. This will include interviewing staff, tracing source documents to accounting records, verifying balances, vouching accounting records to source documents, and comparing accounting records to expectations established during audit planning.

The CPA will evaluate the audit findings and evidence and may request additional information.

Finally, the CPA will prepare required reports and communications and issue an audit draft. The association's management, including the president and treasurer of the board of directors and the association's managing agent, if applicable, will sign a representation letter stating that the financial statements are the responsibility of management and that management's statements to the auditor during the audit process are true. If applicable, the CPA may also present proposed adjusting journal entries that are a part of the draft. The proposed adjusting journal entries should be reviewed and approved by management.

Although the steps above may appear to be sequential, the audit is a continuous process of collecting and analyzing the financial information presented and disclosed in the association's financial statements. Therefore, the audit process may involve repeating steps already taken or asking additional questions after initial answers are received.

Signed Documents Required from CPA

Upon the completion of a financial statement review or audit, the board of director's president and treasurer and the association's managing agent will be required to sign a client representation letter and to review and approve any proposed adjusting journal entries prepared by the CPA.

The client representation letter from the association's management states that all questions and information provided for the review or audit have been answered fully and truthfully and acknowledges that management is responsible for, agrees with, and understands the listed items in the letter.

It is the treasurer's responsibility to ask sufficient questions relating to the information surrounding the proposed adjustments and to perform sufficient due diligence to ascertain the correctness and accuracy of the entries. The treasurer assumes the responsibility of deciding which adjustments to post to the association's books and records. By signing the proposed adjusting journal entries, the treasurer acknowledges that the adjustments are now part of the association's books and that they also should be incorporated in the reviewed or audited financial statements.

Section 17: Incorporation

State statutes may require that condominium associations maintain corporate status. The association's board should review its governing documents for corporate requirements.

Although some state statutes may not require incorporation for condominium or homeowners associations, or those formed prior to a certain date, I recommend that all associations be incorporated with the state and maintain this corporate status to allow the association certain advantages, including protecting the members' individual interests from third-party claims.

To retain the association's corporate status, a report should be filed with the state annually. The association should also record changes to the association's registered agent, changes to the registered address, and changes in the board's president and secretary.

Section 18: Income Tax Matters

Your asociation has two options when it comes time to file your federal income tax return:

Advantages of Filing Form 1120-H	Disadvantages of Filing Form 1120-H
1. Form 1120-H is a simple form to complete.	1. Net nonexempt function income taxed at a flat federal rate of 30 percent.
2. There is less risk of audit.	2. There is no net operating loss deduction allowed.
3. Association is only taxed on net nonexempt function income.	3. Associations cannot write off organizational costs.

1. File as a homeowners association with Form **1120-H**.
2. File as a nonexempt membership organization with Form **1120**.

Below are some guidelines for selecting which form is right for your association in a given year.

Exempt function income: Associations filing a Form 1120-H have the advantage of not being taxed on certain income. This income mainly includes member dues, late fees charged to members, and interest on late member dues.

Nonexempt function income: Nonexempt function income is defined as coming from three main sources: (a) revenue from nonassociation property, (b) revenue from nonmembers for the use of association property, and (c) amounts charged to association members for specific services that are not charged ratably to all members. The first income is from interest income and other commercial ventures that an association operates. The second income is any income that an association receives from nonmembers. The third income includes charges to members for per-use fees, such as for use of a clubhouse or pool.

Advantages of Filing Form 1120	Disadvantages of Filing Form 1120
1. Taxable income is taxed at regular tax rates.	1. There are more rules that need to be followed, which can be time-consuming.
2. Certain tax-planning opportunities may be created by electing Form 1120, including to defer revenue for one year using Revenue Ruling 70-604.	2. Form 1120 is more detailed and more complex and costs more to prepare than Form 1120-H.
3. Net operating losses are allowed.	3. Associations can be taxed on excess member and nonmember income.

Expenses allowed: Nonexempt function income can be offset by expenses that are directly related to that source of nonexempt function income. Other common expenses allowed are accounting fees, management fees, reserve study fees, state income taxes, and bank service charges.

Member vs. nonmember income: Associations that file Form 1120 are required to break their income into categories of member and nonmember. Member income is defined as gross income from members that is used to carry on member functions. Nonmember income is defined as anything that cannot be described as member income. Nonmember income typically comes from interest on investments and any services provided to nonmembers. Unlike for those that file Form 1120-H, associations that file Form 1120 can be taxed on excess member income, which mainly consists of member dues. Form 1120-H treats member dues as exempt, and the dues are not taxed. Associations that file Form 1120 can use Revenue Ruling 70-604 to defer excess membership income to the next year.

Expenses allowed: Nonmember expenses are similar to nonexempt function expenses for associations filing Form 1120-H. The main difference with Form 1120 is that an association also breaks down its expenses between member and nonmember, with adjustments for capital expenditures.

Associations under IRS attack: On October 2, 1995, the IRS published a "deletion's copy" of Tax Advice Memorandum (TAM) No. 9539001 requested by the Jacksonville, Florida, district IRS office relating to the audit of a timeshare association. Even though several years have passed since issuance, this TAM still has authoritative significance and gives added insight into the IRS's position on certain issues relating to filing Form 1120. Does a timeshare audit affect condominium and homeowners associations? The answer appears to be yes. In the eyes of the IRS, all residential associations are the same. When a residential homeowners association files tax Form 1120-H, the IRS considers it a homeowners association. When that same residential association files Form 1120, the IRS considers it a nonexempt membership organization, which is identical to a timeshare association. Associations benefit from filing Form 1120 rather than Form 1120-H because the tax rate for Form 1120 is 15 percent for the first $50,000 of taxable income, compared to a flat rate of 30 percent for Form 1120-H. Associations may elect on an annual basis to file either Form 1120-H or Form 1120. However, filing Form 1120 puts associations at risk if they do not comply with all IRS procedures. The above-mentioned memorandum details numerous failings of the timeshare association, which filed Form 1120, to adhere to IRS procedures.

The following list, borrowed from the winter edition of *The Ledger Quarterly*, addresses the IRS's rulings and describes steps to be taken by associations in order to safely file Form 1120:

- Maintain three separate categories of bank accounts: operating accounts, capital reserve accounts, and noncapital reserve accounts, such as painting and contingency reserves.
- Conduct a reserve study that supports the specific capital use for the reserves.
- Prepare a budget that agrees with the reserve study.
- Separately account for operating and reserve transactions in the association's financial statements and general ledger.
- Have the members annually approve the association's election under Revenue Ruling 70-604. The board of directors may not approve this on behalf of the membership (see appendix C for more).
- The association may not conduct any interfund borrowing between the operating bank accounts and the capital reserve bank accounts.

- If operating and reserve assessments are collected together, deposit them first into the operating account. The reserve dues should than be transferred to the appropriate reserve bank accounts within two weeks.

- Take reserve expenditures directly from the reserve bank accounts. If reserve expenditures are paid from the operating account, that account should be reimbursed in the exact amount of the reserve expenditure at least monthly.

That list describes the association's responsibilities. Tax return preparers should also be aware of additional tax return issues and supporting schedules addressed by this TAM.

Deadlines: All homeowners associations are treated as corporations and have the same deadline of filing two and a half months after their year-end. An association may request a six-month extension of the time to file its return. However, this extension is not an extension to pay tax liability. If an association has tax owed, it is required to make the payment before the two-and-a-half-month deadline after year-end. The IRS will assess penalties and interest on any association that fails to make timely payment of its tax liability.

Penalties: Associations that do not file their tax returns in a timely manner may be penalized 5 percent of the unpaid tax for each month or part of a month the return is late. The maximum penalty that may be assessed for late filing is 25 percent of the unpaid tax. Associations are also penalized on late payment of the tax liability. The penalty for late payment is 0.5 percent of the unpaid tax for each month or part of a month that the tax remains unpaid. The maximum penalty that may be assessed for late payment is 25 percent of the unpaid tax.

Keep in mind that homeowners associations with taxable income may also be liable for state income taxes in those states that have an income tax.

Section 19: Insurance Matters

Most associations are familiar with insurance products that insure the association from loss due to fire, water damage, and personal liability, including officers and directors coverage. Insurance that is sometimes overlooked by associations involves fidelity insurance, which insures the association against loss from dishonesty, embezzlement, and theft by officers, directors, and association employees. This coverage should also include loss from other parties, including contracted community association managers, bookkeepers, and other persons authorized by the association to handle moneys of the association. This coverage is important because many associations have large sums of money in operating and reserve accounts that are potential targets by unscrupulous individuals.

Another insurance coverage that is important if the association uses electronic banking to pay bills or transfer funds is computer fraud insurance. This coverage is different from fidelity insurance. Many banks require that loss from theft due to electronic transactions be reported to the bank within forty-eight hours. If the bank is not notified, the bank is held harmless and will not reimburse the association for losses. Most associations do not have systems in place that alert the board or managing agent in a timely fashion; thus, the bank will not reimburse the association. Computer fraud insurance covers the association in the event of theft due to electronic transactions. The parties covered by this insurance should include officers, directors, association employees, contracted community association managers, bookkeepers, and other persons authorized by the association to handle moneys of the association.

Some fidelity insurance policies include computer fraud insurance. Care should be taken to ensure that the fidelity policy has a computer fraud rider that covers electronic transactions.

Policy coverage on both fidelity and computer fraud insurance should be equal to all reserve account balances plus three months of operating assessments, as well as moneys in other types of funds including remediation funds and contingency funds.

Board members should be familiar with all insurance policies of the association. If board members are unsure of specific provisions of the policies, they should consult with their insurance agent.

The association's treasurer and board of directors should meet annually with the insurance agent. The agent should discuss in layman's terms the insurance coverage, including replacement costs, directors' and officers' liability coverage, and property and liability coverage. The board should question any potential gaps in coverage, as well as how claims are coordinated between the association's policy and individual homeowners' policies. Insurance deductibles should also be reviewed.

Please note that certain financing agencies, such as HUD, require associations to budget for deductibles. I recommend including deductibles in the reserve study.

Section 20: Form 1099—Information Returns

Form 1099 Information Returns

Form 1099 information returns are required to be filed annually when certain conditions are met. Although there are sixteen different 1099 forms, the most commonly used by HOAs are Forms 1099-MISC, 1099-DIV, and 1099-INT. In general, payments for nonemployee compensation, rents, interest, or prizes and awards made in the course of a trade or business transactions aggregating $600 or more are reported on Form 1099-MISC. Payments aggregating $10 or more for dividends, royalties, or pension distributions also require issuance of a Form 1099-Div or 1099-INT.

When filing paper copies of Forms 1099, the recipient copies are required to be mailed by January 31, and the IRS copies are required to be mailed by the end of February. Those filing Forms 1099 electronically have until the end of March to submit the information to the IRS.

Corporate recipients are exempt from receipt of Forms 1099, unless the corporate recipient is an attorney or law firm. Most limited liability companies (LLCs) are not exempt and do need to receive a Form 1099 if they meet the dollar threshold. The IRS applies penalties ranging from $30 to $250 per statement to those failing to file timely or correct returns, and the state may disallow the entire related deduction or issue separate penalties. Some states require electronic submission of certain 1099 Forms if more than ten of any one type are issued.

Form W-9—Request for Taxpayer Identification Number and Certification

Form W-9 is commonly used to request the legal name, type of entity, and identification number of a vendor and is recommended to be completed prior to payment. This form is used for purposes of verifying whether a Form 1099 is required based upon the payee's federal tax classification and provides much of the needed information when preparing Forms 1099 at year-end.

Section 21: Employee vs. Independent Contractor

General Information

The proper classification of workers as employees or independent contractors is crucial. A worker classified as an employee requires income tax withholdings; payroll tax payments (such as FICA, Medicare, and unemployment insurance); preparation and filing of various federal and state payroll returns; and, if eligible, employee benefits such as health insurance, retirement plans, and workers compensation insurance. If a worker is classified as an independent contractor, there is no requirement for payroll tax payments and payroll returns or other employee-type benefits. Generally, the only required filing is an annual Form 1099 (see section 20 for more).

The primary factor in classifying a worker as an employee or independent contractor depends on the extent to which the individual receiving the services has the right to direct and control the actions of the worker with respect to what is done and how it is done.

To determine whether a worker is an independent contractor or an employee, you must examine the relationship between the worker and the business. All evidence of control and independence in this relationship should be considered. The facts that provide this evidence fall into three categories: behavioral control, financial control, and the type of relationship itself (adapted from topic 762 from the Internal Revenue Service website).[1]

Behavioral Control

This covers facts that show if the business has a right to direct and control how the work is done through instructions, training, or other means.

Financial Control

This covers facts that show whether the employer or business has a right to control the business aspects of the worker's job. This includes:

- The extent to which the worker has unreimbursed business expenses
- The extent of the worker's investment in the business
- The extent to which the worker makes services available to the relevant market
- How the business pays the worker
- The extent to which the worker can realize a profit or incur a loss

Facts covered by type of relationship include:

- Written contracts describing the relationship the parties intended to create
- The extent to which the worker is available to perform services for other, similar businesses
- If the business provides the worker with employee-type benefits, such as insurance, a pension plan, vacation pay, or sick pay
- The permanency of the relationship

If it is determined that an employee has been misclassified as an independent contractor, penalties, interest, and payment of withholding taxes on behalf of the employee may result. The extent of penalties and interest depends on whether the misclassification is deemed to be intentional or unintentional.

Section 22: Other Accounting Procedures and Policies to Consider

Periodic Backup of Financial Data

On at least a weekly basis (daily, if possible) the association should prepare a backup of its accounting data files. These backup files should be stored in a location separate from the data source. Having a recent backup of your accounting data allows for the convenient restoration in the event of lost data.

Record Retention Policy

It is recommended that the association establish a record retention policy. An example record retention policy is included in appendix B of this manual. All financial and other records should be stored onsite to avoid the possibility of fragmented records.

Collecting Assessments via a Bank Lockbox

A lockbox is a service offered by many banks that allows owners to mail their payments, along with an encoded payment coupon, directly to the bank. The bank deposits each check directly to the association's bank account (per encoded payment coupon). The bank generates a daily deposit record organized by individual unit and transmits this information to the association electronically or by telephone. Essentially, a lockbox greatly improves the efficiency and accuracy of assessment collections and daily postings. Associations of all sizes can utilize a lockbox.

Fannie Mae Underwriting Requirements

Fannie Mae requirements are relatively straightforward:

- Associations are required to allocate at least 10 percent of total assessments to reserves by depositing the amounts in a reserve bank account. A reserve study prepared by a qualified independent professional company is required for condominium conversion projects. Associations that do not allocate any amounts to reserve funds will most likely not qualify for Fannie Mae financing.

- Fannie Mae also requires that not more than 15 percent of the units be more than sixty days delinquent and that the operating budget provides adequate funds for insurance deductibles.

FHA Certification Requirements

Although FHA loans have similar requirements for down payments and income ratios as Fannie Mae purchased loans, FHA loans are becoming very popular for home buyers due to the fact that these loans have more liberal requirements with respect to a borrower's credit history, making it easier for homebuyers to qualify for financing. HUD has issued guidance for qualifying condominiums to allow buyers and sellers to participate in HUD-insured mortgage products.

HUD requirements include but are not limited to the following requirements for all condominium project approvals:

- Projects with commercial space of between 25 and 35 percent are considered through the HRAP process only.
- Mixed-use condominiums with commercial space of up to 50 percent are considered on a case-by-case basis and must be submitted for review through the Philadelphia Homeownership Center.
- Up to 50 percent of the units may be owned by one investor if at least 50 percent of the total units in the project have been conveyed or are under a bona fide contract for purchase to owner-occupant principal residence purchasers.
- No more than 15 percent of the total units can be in arrears (more than sixty days past due) of the condominium payment.
- At least 50 percent of the total units in an existing project must be sold (includes valid presales).
- At least 50 percent of the total units must be owner occupied or sold to owners who intend to occupy the units.

- Condominium project approvals expire two years from the date the condo was placed on the list of approved condominiums, thus requiring projects to undergo an approval process every two years.
- FHA does not insure any mortgagees after the loan concentration reaches 50 percent.
- Insurance requirements include hazard (master policy), flood (if in flood plain), liability, and fidelity.
- Submission of project documentation should include information on pending litigation, other than routine foreclosures, and special assessments.
- Homeowners association governing documents may not include a legal restriction on conveyance or violate the Fair Housing Act, including a right of first refusal.
- Submission of project documentation should include a signed certification from an authorized representative of the project.
- Homeowners association financial statements for the prior year and for the current year-to-date should show the following:
  - Adequate level of reserves in bank
  - Allocation of at least 10 percent of monthly assessments to reserves
- Homeowners association budgets should show the following:
  - The budget includes allocations and line items to ensure sufficient funds are available to maintain and preserve all amenities and features unique to the condominium project.
  - The budget provides for funding replacement reserves for capital expenditures and deferred maintenance in an account representing at least 10 percent of the budget. In cases where the budgets do not meet these standards, the mortgagee may request a reserve study to assess the financial stability of the project. In such case, the reserve study cannot be more than two years old.

- The budget provides for adequate funding for insurance coverage and deductibles.
- Conversion projects require additional documentation including the following:
  - A professionally prepared reserve study, accompanied by an engineer's report or functional equivalent
  - A reserve deposit balance greater than or equal to the cost of major repairs and replacements included in the reserve study schedule in the next five years

Please note that these approval requirements are subject to change and may have been changed by recently issued guidelines. Associations should work with professionals who specialize in assisting associations with the approval process. It is not recommended that associations apply for approval without consulting with such professionals.

Section 23: FHA Certification and Fannie Mae Underwriting Requirements

Sellers and purchasers of condominiums are becoming aware of the advantages of HUD certification. If an association is approved by HUD for government-insured loans such as FHA loans, the potential purchaser and borrower of a condominium unit has an advantage of using these loans, which may offer easier qualifying ratios and down-payment requirements.

To become approved by HUD, associations need to apply and become recertified periodically. It is strongly recommended that associations work with professionals who specialize in assisting associations with the approval process.

Appendix B:
Record Retention Policy

HOA Record Retention Policy Guidelines

The following is a listing of common records for associations along with recommended retention times from the AICPA. You should check with your attorney or review state statutes to determine if the length of time may be longer.

RECORD	RETENTION GUIDELINE (Paper/Electronic)
Accounting Records:	
Chart of accounts	Permanent
Budgets	Permanent
Invoices/Owner billings	7 years
Vendor bills/expense records	7 years
Accounts payable ledgers	7 years
Accounts receivable ledgers	7 years
Bank statements, cancelled items, and reconciliation reports	7 years
Cancelled checks, important (tax payments, property purchases)	Permanent
Duplicate deposit slips	3 years
Petty-cash records	7 years
Certificate of deposits, matured	7 years
Investments (stocks/bonds), sales, and purchases	Permanent
Balance sheet and profit/loss statement; internal, year-end reports	Permanent
Trial balance, year-end	Permanent
Balance sheet, profit/loss statement; internal, monthly reports	1 year
General ledger report, annual	Permanent
Check register, annual	Permanent
Journal entries	Permanent
Subsidiary ledgers	7 years
Property/Fixed asset purchases	Permanent
Real estate purchases	Permanent
Depreciation schedules	Permanent
Inventory records	7 years
Purchase orders	7 years
Lease payment records	4 years (after term)
Audited/Reviewed/Compiled year-end financial reports	Permanent
Tax returns and IRS documents	Permanent
Tax documents/elections	Permanent

(Continued)

Appendix B

RECORD	RETENTION GUIDELINE (Paper/Electronic)
Employee Records:	
Benefit plans, including pension and profit-sharing plans	Permanent
Employee files, ex-employees	3 years
Payroll checks and register, including time records	7 years
Employment tax returns	Permanent
W-2 forms	Permanent
Employment applications	3 years
Association Documents:	
Ownership/Membership records	Permanent
Deeds, plats, maps	Permanent
Governing documents	Permanent
Declaration, Covenants, Conditions, and Restrictions, including all amendments	Permanent
Articles of Incorporation, including all amendments	Permanent
Bylaws, including all amendments	Permanent
Board policies and resolutions	Permanent
Restrictions and rules	Permanent
Architectural guidelines	Permanent
Architectural approvals and disapprovals	Permanent
Election records	Permanent
Meeting minutes, annual meetings	Permanent
Meeting minutes, board of director	Permanent
Meeting minutes, committees	Permanent
Other Documents:	
Insurance policies	4 years (after term)
Insurance claims	Permanent
Contracts, vendor, minor	4 years (after term)
Contracts, vendor, major	Permanent
Contracts, employee	Permanent
Contracts, management	Permanent
Bids/Proposals	3 years
Correspondence, general	3 years
Correspondence, legal matters*	Permanent
Leases	4 years (after term)
Mortgages	Permanent
Note payable documentation	4 years (after term)

*Check with your attorney prior to discarding records that may be related to pending litigation.

Appendix C:
Example Documents—Resolutions and Policies and 70-604 Election Letter Recommended Format

Example of Competitive Bidding Policy

[NAME OF ASSOCIATION]

Resolution of the Board of Directors

COMPETITIVE BIDDING POLICY

Resolved, management will place out to bid [from time to time, as specified by the board], whenever practical, a minimum of two and a maximum of three bids for the work for repairs and maintenance as required by the association. The value of work to be placed out to bid will be in excess of [$X,XXX].

ATTEST:
[Name of Association]

_____

President
Date: _____

_____

Secretary
Date: _____

Resolution of the Board of Directors of [Name of Association]

Example of Interfund Borrowing Repayment Plan

[NAME OF ASSOCIATION]

Resolution of the Board of Directors

INTERFUND BORROWING REPAYMENT PLAN

As of December 31, 20[XX], [$XXX,XXX] of replacement reserve assessments and [$X,XXX] of working capital contributions had been borrowed to pay for operating expenses.

Resolved, the association plans to repay the amounts due to the replacement fund and working capital fund as follows: [Repayment plan to be entered here].

ATTEST:
[Name of Association]

_____

President
Date: _____

_____

Secretary
Date: _____

Resolution of the Board of Directors of [Name of Association]

Example of Investment Policy

[NAME OF ASSOCIATION]

Resolution of the Board of Directors

INVESTMENT POLICY

The association's investment objective is to earn as much as possible while protecting the association's principal.

Resolved, funds deposited in any one financial institution will not exceed $250,000, which is the maximum balance insured by the Federal Deposit Insurance Corporation (FDIC) at each financial institution, and

Resolved, if the rate of return on certificates of deposit (CDs) exceeds the rate of return on money market accounts, the association will move funds to CDs and will ladder the CDs to ensure the availability of cash when needed.

ATTEST:
[Name of Association]

_____
President
Date: _____

_____
Secretary
Date: _____

Resolution of the Board of Directors of [Name of Association]

70-604 Election Letter Recommended Format

ASSOCIATION RESOLUTION FOR REVENUE RULING 70-604 ELECTION—EXCESS INCOME APPLIED TO THE FOLLOWING YEAR'S ASSESSMENTS

RESOLUTION MUST BE VOTED ON BY THE MEMBERSHIP AT THE ANNUAL MEETING

ANNUAL RESOLUTION OF THE _____ [NAME] _____

RE: EXCESS INCOME APPLIED TO THE FOLLOWING YEAR'S ASSESSMENTS REVENUE RULING 70-604

WHEREAS, the _____ [NAME] _____ is a [name of state] corporation duly organized and existing under the laws of the State of [name of state]; and

WHEREAS, the members desire that the corporation shall act in full accordance with the rulings and regulations of the Internal Revenue Service;

NOW, THEREFORE, the members hereby adopt the following resolution by and on behalf of the _____ [NAME] _____:

RESOLVED, that any excess of membership income over membership expenses for the year ended _____ [DATE] _____ shall be applied against the subsequent tax year member assessments as provided by IRS Revenue Ruling 70-604.

This resolution was voted on and made a part of the minutes of the annual meeting of _____ [DATE] _____.

BY: _____
President

ATTESTED: _____
Secretary

Treasurer's Note: This election should be voted on at the annual meeting. The vote does not require a quorum. This election does not bind the association in filing a particular tax form. It does, however, make it safer to file Form 1120 if the association so desires.

Appendix D:
Example Chart of Accounts
for Homeowners Associations

Associations have very specific accounting and reporting characteristics. It is not practical to use a chart of accounts (a listing of balance sheet and income and expense categories and related numbering for accounting systems) that for-profit businesses use to keep track of day-to-day income and expense transactions.

The following chart gives a representative chart of accounts that may be helpful to use when performing bookkeeping for community associations:

Account Number	Description	Type
10100	Cash in Bank—Operating Checking	Asset
10200	Cash in Bank—Operating Money Market	Asset
10300	Investments—Operating CDs	Asset
10310	Unamortized Premium/Discount on Investments—Operating	Asset
10400	Petty Cash	Asset
10500	Cash in Bank—Operating Payroll	Asset
11110	Interfund Balance—Due from Operating to Replacement Reserve	Asset
11120	Interfund Balance—Due from Operating to Working Capital	Asset
11130	Interfund Balance—Due from Operating to Special Assessment	Asset
11140	Interfund Balance—Due from Operating to Litigation	Asset
12110	Accounts Receivable—Assessments—Operating	Asset
12210	Accounts Receivable—Assessments—Replacement Reserves	Asset
12120	Accounts Receivable—Assessments—Developer Operating	Asset
12220	Accounts Receivable—Assessments—Developer Replacement Reserves	Asset
12310	Accounts Receivable—Special Assessments	Asset

(Continued)

Appendix D

Account Number	Description	Type
12410	Accounts Receivable—Working Capital Contributions	Asset
12420	Accounts Receivable—Working Capital Contributions—Developer	Asset
12510	Litigation Proceeds Receivable	Asset
12610	Accounts Receivable—Architectural Control Fees	Asset
12620	Accounts Receivable—Reimbursements	Asset
12630	Accounts Receivable—Other	Asset
13100	Prepaid Insurance	Asset
13200	Prepaid Expenses	Asset
13310	Prepaid Federal Tax	Asset
13320	Prepaid State Tax (not applicable in some states)	Asset
13330	Prepaid Property Tax	Asset
13400	Deferred Expenses	Asset
14110	Automobile	Asset
14120	Accumulated Depreciation on Automobile	Asset
14210	Capital Improvements	Asset
14220	Accumulated Depreciation on Capital Improvements	Asset
14310	Equipment/Furnishings	Asset
14320	Accumulated Depreciation on Equipment/Furnishings	Asset
14410	Other Fixed Assets per Association's Capitalization Policy	Asset
14420	Accumulated Depreciation on Other Fixed Assets	Asset
14510	Land	Asset
15100	Cash in Bank—Replacement Reserve Checking	Asset
15200	Cash in Bank—Replacement Reserve Money Market	Asset
15300	Investments—Replacement Reserve CDs	Asset
15310	Unamortized Premium/Discount on Investments—Replacement Reserve	Asset
11210	Interfund Balance—Due from Replacement Reserve to Operating	Asset
11220	Interfund Balance—Due from Replacement Reserve to Working Capital	Asset
11230	Interfund Balance—Due from Replacement Reserve to Special Assessment	Asset
11240	Interfund Balance—Due from Replacement Reserve to Litigation	Asset
16100	Cash in Bank—Working Capital Checking	Asset
16200	Cash in Bank—Working Capital Money Market	Asset
16300	Investments—Working Capital CDs	Asset
16310	Unamortized Premium/Discount on Investments—Working Capital	Asset

(Continued)

Appendix D

Account Number	Description	Type
11310	Interfund Balance—Due from Working Capital to Operating	Asset
11320	Interfund Balance—Due from Working Capital to Replacement Reserve	Asset
11330	Interfund Balance—Due from Working Capital to Special Assessment	Asset
11340	Interfund Balance—Due from Working Capital to Litigation	Asset
17100	Cash in Bank—Special Assessment Checking	Asset
17200	Cash in Bank—Special Assessment Money Market	Asset
17300	Investments—Special Assessment CDs	Asset
17310	Unamortized Premium/Discount on Investments—Special Assessment	Asset
11410	Interfund Balance—Due from Special Assessment to Operating	Asset
11420	Interfund Balance—Due from Special Assessment to Replacement Reserve	Asset
11430	Interfund Balance—Due from Special Assessment to Working Capital	Asset
11440	Interfund Balance—Due from Special Assessment to Litigation	Asset
20100	Accounts Payable—Operating	Liability
20110	Accrued Accounts Payable—Operating	Liability
20120	Payroll Payable	Liability
20130	Insurance Proceeds Payable	Liability
20210	Federal Tax Payable	Liability
20220	State Tax Payable (not applicable in some states)	Liability
20230	Property Tax payable	Liability
20300	Refundable Deposits	Liability
21100	Accounts Payable—Replacement Reserves	Liability
21110	Accrued Accounts Payable—Replacement Reserves	Liability
22100	Accounts Payable—Special Assessments	Liability
22110	Accrued Accounts Payable—Special Assessments	Liability
23100	Accounts Payable—Litigation	Liability
23110	Accrued Accounts Payable—Litigation	Liability
24100	Line of Credit Payable	Liability
24210	Note Payable—Current Portion	Liability
24220	Note Payable—Long Term Portion	Liability
25100	Prepaid Assessments—Operating	Liability
25200	Prepaid Assessments—Operating—Developer	Liability
26100	Prepaid Assessments—Replacement Reserve	Liability
26200	Prepaid Assessments—Replacement Reserve—Developer	Liability

(Continued)

Account Number	Description	Type
27000	Prepaid Assessments—Special Assessments	Liability
28000	Deferred Revenue—Special Assessments	Liability
29000	Deferred Revenue—Litigation	Liability
30000	Operating Fund	Fund Balance
31000	Replacement Reserve Fund	Fund Balance
32100	Working Capital Fund	Fund Balance
32200	Current Year Working Capital Contributions	Fund Balance
33000	Special Assessment Fund	Fund Balance
34000	Litigation Fund	Fund Balance
30100	Transfer from Operating to Replacement Reserves	Fund Balance
30200	Transfer from Operating to Special Assessment	Fund Balance
30300	Transfer from Operating to Litigation	Fund Balance
32100	Transfer from Working Capital to Operating	Fund Balance
32200	Transfer from Working Capital to Replacement Reserves	Fund Balance
32300	Transfer from Working Capital to Special Assessment	Fund Balance
32400	Transfer from Working Capital to Litigation	Fund Balance
33100	Transfer from Special Assessment to Operating	Fund Balance
33200	Transfer from Special Assessment to Replacement Reserves	Fund Balance
33300	Transfer from Special Assessment to Litigation	Fund Balance
34100	Transfer from Litigation to Operating	Fund Balance
34200	Transfer from Litigation to Replacement Reserves	Fund Balance
34300	Transfer from Litigation to Special Assessment	Fund Balance
40100	Operating Assessments	Operating Revenue
40200	Operating Assessments—Developer	Operating Revenue
41000	Interest Income—Operating	Operating Revenue
42100	Late Fees	Operating Revenue
42200	Interest on Late Assessments	Operating Revenue
43000	Architectural Control Fees	Operating Revenue
44100	Rental Income	Operating Revenue
44200	Laundry Income	Operating Revenue
44300	Key Income	Operating Revenue
44400	Tax Refund	Operating Revenue
44500	Advertising Income	Operating Revenue
44600	Vending Machine Income	Operating Revenue
44700	Cell Phone Tower Income	Operating Revenue
44800	Lease Income	Operating Revenue
45000	Miscellaneous Income	Operating Revenue
50010	Appliance Maintenance & Repair—Operating	Operating Expenses
50020	Automobile Gasoline	Operating Expenses
50030	Automobile Maintenance & Repair—Operating	Operating Expenses
50040	Backflow Testing	Operating Expenses

(Continued)

Account Number	Description	Type
50050	Bark dust	Operating Expenses
50060	Boiler Maintenance & Repair—Operating	Operating Expenses
50070	Building Maintenance & Repair—Operating	Operating Expenses
50080	Carpet Cleaning	Operating Expenses
50090	Carpet Repairs	Operating Expenses
50100	Carport Maintenance & Repair—Operating	Operating Expenses
50110	Chimney Maintenance & Repair—Operating	Operating Expenses
50120	Dock Maintenance & Repair—Operating	Operating Expenses
50130	Drainage Maintenance & Repair—Operating	Operating Expenses
50140	Elevator—Other	Operating Expenses
50150	Elevator Contract	Operating Expenses
50160	Emergency Contingency	Operating Expenses
50170	Exterior Maintenance & Repair—Operating	Operating Expenses
50180	Fences Maintenance & Repair—Operating	Operating Expenses
50190	Fire Protection Maintenance & Repair—Operating	Operating Expenses
50200	Floors Maintenance & Repair—Operating	Operating Expenses
50210	Garage Maintenance & Repair—Operating	Operating Expenses
50220	Gutter/Downspout Maintenance & Repair—Operating	Operating Expenses
50230	HVAC—Other Maintenance & Repair—Operating	Operating Expenses
50240	HVAC Contract	Operating Expenses
50250	Interior Maintenance & Repair—Operating	Operating Expenses
50260	Irrigation Maintenance & Repair—Operating	Operating Expenses
50270	Janitorial—Contract	Operating Expenses
50280	Janitorial—Supplies	Operating Expenses
50290	Landscape—Payroll Taxes	Operating Expenses
50300	Landscape—Contract	Operating Expenses
50310	Landscape—Improvements	Operating Expenses
50320	Landscape—Payroll	Operating Expenses
50330	Laundry Machine Maintenance & Repair—Operating	Operating Expenses
50340	Light Fixtures Maintenance & Repair—Operating	Operating Expenses
50350	Maintenance Staff—Payroll	Operating Expenses
50360	Maintenance Staff—Payroll Taxes	Operating Expenses
50370	Painting Maintenance & Repair—Operating	Operating Expenses
50380	Parking & Street Cleaning	Operating Expenses
50390	Paths/Sidewalks Maintenance & Repair—Operating	Operating Expenses
50400	Patio/Deck Maintenance & Repair—Operating	Operating Expenses
50410	Pest Control	Operating Expenses
50420	Plant Maintenance & Repair—Operating	Operating Expenses
50430	Plumbing Maintenance & Repair—Operating	Operating Expenses

(Continued)

Account Number	Description	Type
50440	Pond Maintenance & Repair—Operating	Operating Expenses
50450	Pool/Spa—Supplies	Operating Expenses
50460	Pool/Spa Maintenance—Contract	Operating Expenses
50470	Pump Maintenance & Repair—Operating	Operating Expenses
50480	Roof Maintenance & Repair—Operating	Operating Expenses
50490	Security Gate Maintenance & Repair—Operating	Operating Expenses
50500	Security System Maintenance & Repair—Operating	Operating Expenses
50510	Siding Maintenance & Repair—Operating	Operating Expenses
50520	Stairwells Maintenance & Repair—Operating	Operating Expenses
50530	Supplies for Maintenance & Repair—Operating	Operating Expenses
50540	Tree Pruning/Spraying	Operating Expenses
50550	Vending Machine Maintenance & Repair—Operating	Operating Expenses
50560	Water Lines Maintenance & Repair—Operating	Operating Expenses
50570	Window Cleaning	Operating Expenses
51010	Cable TV	Operating Expenses
51020	Dumpster	Operating Expenses
51030	Electricity	Operating Expenses
51040	Elevator Telephone	Operating Expenses
51050	Garbage	Operating Expenses
51060	Gas	Operating Expenses
51070	Oil	Operating Expenses
51080	Sewer	Operating Expenses
51090	Telephone	Operating Expenses
51100	Water	Operating Expenses
51110	Water/Sewer	Operating Expenses
51120	Accounting	Operating Expenses
51130	Administrator—Payroll	Operating Expenses
51140	Administrator—Payroll Taxes	Operating Expenses
51150	Annual Meeting Expenses	Operating Expenses
51160	Art/Flowers	Operating Expenses
51170	Audit/Review	Operating Expenses
51180	Bad Debt	Operating Expenses
51190	Bank Fees	Operating Expenses
51200	Bank Fees on Loan/Note	Operating Expenses
51210	Depreciation	Operating Expenses
51220	Employee Benefits	Operating Expenses
51230	Equipment Leases	Operating Expenses
51240	Income Tax	Operating Expenses
51250	Gain/Loss on Sale of Asset	Operating Expenses
51260	Insurance	Operating Expenses
51270	Interest on Loan/Note Payable	Operating Expenses

(Continued)

Account Number	Description	Type
51280	Legal	Operating Expenses
51290	License/Fees	Operating Expenses
51300	Miscellaneous	Operating Expenses
51310	Office	Operating Expenses
51320	Operations	Operating Expenses
51330	Property Tax	Operating Expenses
51340	Rental Expenses	Operating Expenses
51350	Tax Preparation	Operating Expenses
51360	Website	Operating Expenses
52010	Management—Contract	Operating Expenses
52020	Management—Payroll	Operating Expenses
52030	Management—Payroll Taxes	Operating Expenses
52040	Reserve Study Consultants	Operating Expenses
52050	Security—Contract	Operating Expenses
60100	Replacement Reserve Assessments	Reserve Revenue
60200	Replacement Reserve Assessments—Developer	Reserve Revenue
61000	Interest Income—Replacement Reserves	Reserve Revenue
65010	Administration Expenses Related to Replacement Reserves	Reserve Expenses
65020	Bank Fees	Reserve Expenses
66010	Bark Dust	Reserve Expenses
66020	Carpet	Reserve Expenses
66030	Carport	Reserve Expenses
66040	Chimney	Reserve Expenses
66050	Consultants	Reserve Expenses
66060	Contingency	Reserve Expenses
66070	Dock	Reserve Expenses
66080	Doors	Reserve Expenses
66090	Elevator	Reserve Expenses
66100	Fences	Reserve Expenses
66110	Floors	Reserve Expenses
66120	Garage	Reserve Expenses
66130	Gutters/Downspout	Reserve Expenses
66140	HVAC	Reserve Expenses
66150	Interior	Reserve Expenses
66160	Irrigation	Reserve Expenses
66170	Landscape	Reserve Expenses
66180	Painting	Reserve Expenses
66190	Paths/Sidewalks	Reserve Expenses
66200	Patio/Deck	Reserve Expenses
66210	Paving & Curbs	Reserve Expenses
66220	Plumbing	Reserve Expenses
66230	Pool/Spa	Reserve Expenses

(Continued)

Account Number	Description	Type
66240	Road	Reserve Expenses
66250	Roof	Reserve Expenses
66260	Security Gate	Reserve Expenses
66270	Security System	Reserve Expenses
66280	Siding Stairwells	Reserve Expenses
66290	Signs	Reserve Expenses
66300	Storeroom	Reserve Expenses
66310	Tree Pruning/Spraying	Reserve Expenses
66320	Tree Replacement	Reserve Expenses
66330	Windows	Reserve Expenses
70100	Special Assessments	Other Revenue
71000	Interest Income—Special Assessments	Other Revenue
75010	Administration Expenses Related to Special Assessment	Other Expenses
75020	Bank Fees—Related to Special Assessment	Other Expenses
76010	Expenses Related to Special Assessment	Other Expenses
75030	Interest on Loan/Note Payable—Special Assessment	Other Expenses
80100	Litigation Proceeds	Other Revenue
81000	Interest Income—Litigation Proceeds	Other Revenue
85010	Administration Expenses Related to Litigation	Other Expenses
85020	Bank Fees—Related to Litigation	Other Expenses
86010	Consultants Expense Related to Litigation	Other Expenses
85030	Interest on Loan/Note Payable—Litigation	Other Expenses
86020	Legal Expenses Related to Litigation	Other Expenses
86030	Other Expenses Related to Litigation	Other Expenses
91000	Interest Income—Working Capital	Other Revenue
95000	Working Capital Expenditures	Other Expenses

Appendix E:
Reserve Funding and the Risk
Mitigation Matrix

R eserve studies involve two distinct phases: the physical analysis and the funding analysis. The physical analysis includes, but is not limited to, determining the association's legal responsibility of repairing, replacing, and maintaining association property (components) and identifying each component and its condition, cost, and useful life. The funding analysis includes preparing a funding model that considers the cost and frequency of repairs, replacements, and maintenance procedures. This funding model includes provisions for inflation on future expenditures, interest earned on reserves, and income taxes.

The theory behind funding is simple: determine how much money the association should set aside in the replacement reserve bank account each year so there is always enough money to pay for needed repair, replacement, and maintenance expenses and assess accordingly. Since this funding model is based on numerous assumptions, many association professionals prefer to include a contingency amount in the funding model. Although the theory of funding is relatively simple, the calculation of the required contribution to reserves is complicated by the various methods of funding and the determination of the appropriate contingency. For purposes of this book, *contingency* is defined as "the amount of cash set aside in the replacement reserve over and above the calculated amount needed to fund 100 percent of needed expenditures." In other words, it is extra cash to fund unbudgeted expenditures or "surprises."

Community Association Institute (CAI) Reserve Specialist and Association of Professional Reserve Analyst standards include three acceptable funding models: baseline, threshold, and fully funded models. (Note that there are other terms that describe these models. For the sake of simplicity, I am using the above terms).

The baseline method involves preparing a funding model that funds all expected costs over a specified period, in many cases thirty years. Although this model funds the replacement reserve bank account for all expected costs, it does *not* include a contingency amount should any components cost more than expected. Proponents of this method want to fund only expected costs to maintain, repair, and replace common area components. Note that this model is the bare minimum of funding and assumes there will be no surprises. Over a thirty-year period, the baseline funding model would show a cash flow projection that funds all expenditures, and at some point the cash balance in the replacement fund bank account would drop close to a zero balance and then start building cash for the next major expenditure. The year the cash balance drops close to zero is risky to the association since there is no extra cash to pay for surprises.

The threshold method involves preparing a funding model that funds all expected costs much like the baseline method but also includes a contingency amount for surprises. Reserve study specialists refer to this contingency as the "threshold." The threshold method provides an amount that the projected replacement reserve cash balance will not fall below, say $100,000. The $100,000 is called the threshold and provides needed funds to pay for surprises. Proponents of this method realize that over a thirty-year period, unexpected costs may arise, and it may be prudent to have extra cash to pay for these surprises. The challenge for reserve study providers is determining the amount of the threshold or extra cash.

The fully funded method uses a formula for computing the threshold. This formula mirrors the method used for computing depreciation. It computes a threshold that in some cases allows funding for twice the amount of expected costs. Knowing that the fully funded method, if 100 percent funded, provides for a very large threshold, reserve study providers often use a funding target of less than 100 percent. Please note that the higher the percentage funded, the more extra cash is kept in the replacement reserve bank account as a contingency, over and above the amount necessary to pay for all expected repairs and replacements.

The following graph illustrates the level of extra cash built into each model:

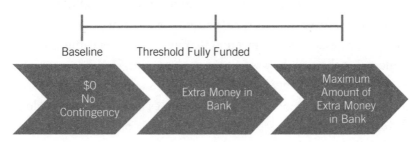

Graph I: Methods of Funding in Relation to Extra Cash (Contingency)

Risk of Special Assessment

Many reserve study professionals present statistics that show the risk of a special assessment based on the percentage funded. For instance, if an association is 50 percent funded, these statistics indicate there will be an 11.6 percent chance of a special assessment. The higher the percentage funded, the lower the potential of a special assessment. Please be aware that these statistics have been compiled by a reserve study provider and not vetted by CAI. However, if the contention is that the more extra cash an association has in the bank, the less likely the association will be to special assess due to surprises, then the underlying theory appears reasonable.

If your funding goal is to fund for all expected expenditures and to allow funding for surprises, how can you mitigate the risk of surprises, thus lowering the contingency amount?

What are some of the surprises that associations experience?

- The design, materials, or workmanship on original construction is not adequate, thus requiring repairs or remediation, or may result in a significant reduction in the estimated useful lives of components. A complete building envelope inspection may catch issues early on that may reduce the cost of repairs and may allow the association to bring an action against the developer or contractor. This investigation may include intrusive openings around decks, windows, roofs, and siding.
- The association does not adequately maintain the components, which may lead to unexpected repairs or significantly reduced estimated useful lives. A maintenance plan consistently followed by the association may help components last longer with fewer repairs.
- The association does not perform ongoing inspections of components. Ongoing inspections may catch issues before they become worse and cost more to repair.
- The reserve study does not include all components that need to be funded. Missing components may include plumbing and irrigation systems; water and sewer lines; dry rot; windows and doors; deck assemblies; asphalt; major landscaping projects; concrete issues, including spalling and rusted rebar; and replacement of siding and trim. Failure to include all components will likely lead to a special assessment to pay for unbudgeted repairs.
- The reserve study is not updated annually to account for increase in prices, changes in cash reserves, application of adjusted inflation in funding model, or change in estimated useful lives.

Failure to update the reserve study on an annual basis may lead to unbudgeted expenditures.

- The RFP (request for proposal) for repair and replacement projects is not written correctly, resulting in specifications that either are inadequate or do not address issues. Using a construction professional to assist with RFPs can help ensure that repair and replacement projects are performed by qualified professionals and include all needed costs and procedures.
- The association does not use a construction consultant on major projects to ensure that work is performed properly. The danger of not using a consultant increases the likelihood the person hired will use substandard materials and workmanship and increases the possibility of re-repairing or replacing the components or may significantly reduce estimated useful lives.

Since it appears that the threshold and fully funded models expect surprises, should associations that have procedures that address the risk of surprises be governed by the same funding rules as associations that do not?

Many reserve study providers recommend a percentage funded of at least 70 percent. The matrix below shows that if associations follow best practices in maintaining common area components, the percentage funded could be much lower because the likelihood of a surprise is diminished. Note that this matrix addresses the fully funded percentage but can also be used as a tool to determine the required threshold using the threshold method.

Associations that adopt best practice procedures and spend a little more each year on maintenance, inspections, reserve study updates, and construction oversight can reduce the amount that is assessed to overfund the replacement reserve bank account to pay for unexpected costs.

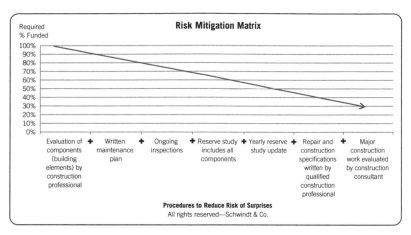

Graph II: Best Practices in Relation to the Need to Overfund

As always, associations should look to the credentialed reserve study provider for guidance.

Further Reading

- Community Associations Network website[1]
- Community Associations Institute website[2]
- Robert McConnell HOA Parliamentarian website[3]
- National Association of Housing Cooperatives website[4]

Appendix F:
Typical Board Meeting Agenda

Happy Homeowners Board Meeting
October 24, 2015

- Open Forum: 9:30 AM [A forum before meeting commences to allow members to address the board with issues. The board should listen and need not respond. Each member's issue presentation is generally limited to two to five minutes.]
- Call to Order: 10:00 AM
- Determination of Quorum
- Review/Accept Minutes of Previous Meeting
- Treasurer's Report
- Committee Reports
- Unfinished Business
    a. Redesign of Children's Play Area
- New Business
    a. Tennis Court Repairs
- Executive Session: Year-End Bonuses and Salaries
- Close of Executive Session and Reconvene
- Review of Action Items
- Set Date of Next Meeting
- Adjournment

NOTE: No decisions are made during the executive session. Results (i.e., decisions) may be set out before the end of the meeting or during the next meeting when in open session. As the example is for year-end bonuses, if the meeting is in November, the decision could be made (motion, vote) in December or before the close of the November meeting.

Here is an example of typical minutes for the meeting agenda given previously:

Happy Homeowners Association
Minutes of the Board Meeting of October 24, 2015

Open Forum:

The chair recognized homeowners present for the Open Forum at 9:30 AM.

Five homeowners were present: Anne Baker, Charlie Davis, Erin Forrest, Gene Harding, and Ian Josephson.

Anne asked if the option to have seal coating done on driveways was still open.

Anne noted that there appeared to be tent caterpillars in the bushes next to the swings in the common area.

Charlie Fran noted her approval of the painting contractors and commended them on their cleanup after painting her unit.

The chair called the meeting to order at 10:00 AM.

Present were Sarah Rogers, Uma Thornton, Wally Verbin, Melvin Laird, and the chair, Zelda Young. Absent were Larry Kerns (vacation) and Pat O'Brien.

Quorum was noted.

Sarah moved that the minutes of the last meeting be accepted. Uma seconded. There was no discussion; the motion passed unanimously.

Wally presented the treasurer's report. Melvin moved that the report be accepted; Uma seconded. There was no discussion; the motion passed unanimously.

The architectural committee reported that they had received a request from a homeowner to install a metal-and-glass fencing around an upper deck, but as the materials were not outlined, they had returned the request to the owner, seeking clarification.

The grounds committee reported that there were three bids received for repairs to the tennis court, and recommended that the bid from It's a Racket be accepted by the board.

In unfinished business, it was noted that due to inclement weather, the walkthrough scheduled with vendors for a redesign of the children's play area had been postponed from two weeks ago until next Tuesday. Uma moved that the board make a final decision at the next meeting. There was no second, and the motion died.

New Business: Wally moved that the bid from It's a Racket be accepted, and Sarah seconded. In discussion, it was noted that the bid was the highest bid, but that it included a recoating of the tennis court surface every other year, in 2017 and 2019, and replacement of the benches. Melvin moved to amend the motion "to include benches not to exceed the quoted price, subject to board review of lesser cost benches with commensurate reduction in final cost." Sarah seconded the motion.

After discussion that the proposed benches of teak would require significant maintenance and the cost was unknown, the chair called for a vote on the amendment. The amendment passed unanimously.

The chair called for discussion of the main motion. After discussion, Melvin moved to postpone the vote until the next meeting. Sarah seconded. There being no discussion, the chair called for a vote to postpone deciding on the contract. The vote was unanimous.

The meeting was suspended at 10:52 AM as the board went into Executive Session.

The meeting was reconvened at 11:26 AM.

The chair noted the action items: all board members were to review alternatives to tennis court benches prior to the next meeting, and Melvin, liaison with the ARC committee, was to confirm that the committee was careful to watch all timelines for responses.

A motion was made by Sarah to set a work session for November 11 at 6:30 PM to review the proposed operating budget and proposed reserve budget prior to the usual November meeting. Uma seconded the motion. There being no discussion, the chair called for the vote. The motion passed unanimously.

A motion was made by Melvin to set the regular board meeting for November 24th. Sarah seconded the motion. There being no discussion, the chair called for the vote. The motion passed unanimously.

There being no further business, Wally moved the meeting be adjourned, and Uma seconded. There being no discussion, the chair called for the vote. It passed unanimously. The meeting adjourned at 11:47 AM.

Notes

Chapter 4

1. Peter M. Dunbar, Esq., and Marc W. Dunbar, Esq., *The Homeowners Association Manual* (Sarasota, FL: Pineapple Press, Inc., 2004).
2. Gary A. Poliakoff, *The Law of Condominium Operations* (New York, NY: Clark Boardman Callaghan, 1991).
3. Wayne S. Hyatt and Susan F. French, *Community Association Law: Cases and Materials on Common Interest Communities*, second edition (Durham, NC: Carolina Academic Press, 2008).
4. Peter M. Dunbar, Esq., *The Condominium Concept: A Practical Guide for Officers, Owners, Realtors, Attorneys, and Directors of Florida Condominiums*, thirteenth edition (Sarasota, FL: Pineapple Press, Inc., 2012).

Chapter 5

1. Gary A. Poliakoff and Ryan Poliakoff, *New Neighborhoods: The Consumer's Guide to Condominium, Co-op, and HOA Living* (Austin, TX: Emerald Book Company, 2009).

Chapter 6

1. Debra H. Lewin and Ellen De Haan, *Self-Management: A Guide for the Small Community Association,* second edition (Alexandria, VA: Community Associations Institute Press, 2001).
2. Michael E. Packard, *GAP Report: Choosing a Management Company,* fifth edition (Alexandria, VA: Community Associations Institute Press, 2002).

Chapter 7

1. David J. Minahan, "Corporation and Security Law: State and Federal Regulation of Condominiums," *Marquette Law Review* 58, no. 1 (1975).
2. Donna S. Bennett, "Condominium Homeownership in the United States: A Selected Annotated Bibliography of Legal Sources," *Law Library Journal* 103, no. 2 (2011–16).

Chapter 9

1. "How to Take Minutes," WikiHow, accessed August 30, 2015, http://www .wikihow.com/take-minutes

Chapter 10

1. "Robert's Rules of Order," Rulesonline.com, accessed August 30, 2015, http:// www.rulesonline.com
2. Clifford J. Treese, *Managing & Governing: How Community Associations Function,* (Falls Church, VA: Community Associations Institute Press, 2007).

Chapter 11

1. Mary Avgerinos, *Conflict Resolution: How ADR Helps Community Associations* (Alexandria, VA: Community Associations Institute Press, 2004).
2. Dana Caspersen and Joost Elffers, *Changing the Conversation: The 17 Principles of Conflict Resolution* (London, UK: Profile Books Ltd, 2015).

Chapter 14

1. "Treasurer's Handbook," Schwindt & Co. website, accessed August 30, 2015, https://www.schwindtco.com/resources/treasurers-handbook

Chapter 16

1. *Best Practices Report #1: Reserve Studies/Management* (Falls Church, VA: Foundation for Community Association Research, 2014).
2. Mitchell H. Frumkin, PE, CGP, and Nico F. March, CFM, RRP, *Reserve Funds: How & Why Community Associations Invest Assets* (Alexandria, VA: Community Associations Institute Press, 2005).

Chapter 18

1. Ross W. Feinberg, Esq., and Ronald L. Perl, Esq., *Construction Defect Litigation: The Community Association's Guide to the Legal Process* (Alexandria, VA: Community Associations Institute Press, 2006).
2. Thomas E. Miller, Rachel M. Miller, and Mathew T. Miller, *Home and Condo Defects: A Consumer Guide to Faulty Construction*, second edition (Santa Ana, CA: Seven Locks Press, 2012).

Chapter 22

1. Allen Kelley, *RCI Points User Guide: Tips, Tricks and Secrets: A Practical Guide to Understanding and Using RCI Points* (n.p.: author, 2011).
2. Vincent Lehr, *Timeshare Tips & Tricks: Stay at 5 Star Resorts for Pennies, Eliminate Maintenance Costs, Trade, and What to Do When You Don't Want It Anymore* (Seattle, WA: SIG, LLC, 2011).

Chapter 24

1. Adam Bonislawski, "Million-Dollar Mobile Homes," *Wall Street Journal*, August 7 2014, http://www.wsj.com/articles/million-dollar-mobile-homes-1407431698

Chapter 26

1. Fellowship for Intentional Community, http://www.ic.org

Appendix A, Section 21

1. Internal Revenue Service, "Topic 762—Independent Contractor vs. Employee," accessed May 27, 2015, http://www.irs.gov/taxtopics/tc762.html

Appendix E

1. Community Associations Network, http://communityassociations.net
2. Community Associations Institute, http://www.caionline.org
3. Robert McConnell Productions: Parliamentary Procedure Resource, http://www.parli.com
4. National Association of Housing Cooperatives (NAHC), http://coophousing.org